Prentice Hall **Realidades A**

Communication Workbook with Test Preparation

PEARSON

Boston, Massachusetts Chandler, Arizona Glenview, Illinois Upper Saddle River, New Jersey

Art and Map Credits
Page 124: (map) Jennifer Thermes; **Page 136:** (map) Jennifer Thermes; **Page 142:** Eldon Doty/H.K. Portfolio, Inc.; **Page 148:** Ted Smykal; **Page 154:** (map) Design Associates; **Page 160:** © Eldon Doty/H.K. Portfolio, Inc.

ISBN-13: 978-0-13-322574-7
ISBN-10: 0-13-322574-7
1 2 3 4 5 6 7 8 9 10 V0N4 16 15 14 13 12

PEARSON

Table of Contents

Writing, Audio & Video Activities

Boston, Massachusetts Chandler, Arizona Glenview, Illinois Upper Saddle River, New Jersey

Table of Contents

Tema 3: La comida

Tema 4: Los pasatiempos

Capítulo 4A: ¿Adónde vas?

Capítulo 4B: ¿Quieres ir conmigo?

Nombre ______________________ Hora ________

Fecha ______________________

AUDIO

Actividad 1

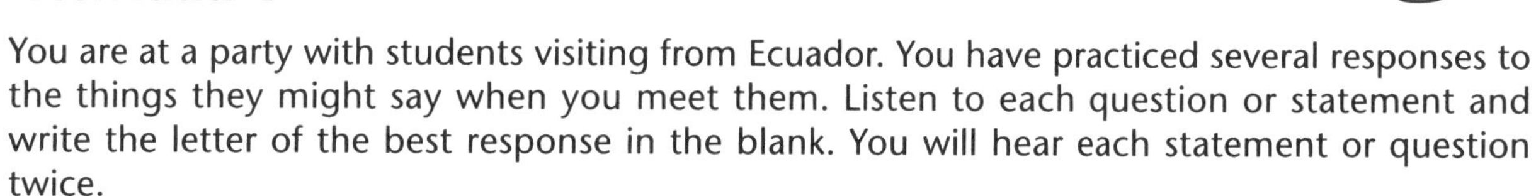

You are at a party with students visiting from Ecuador. You have practiced several responses to the things they might say when you meet them. Listen to each question or statement and write the letter of the best response in the blank. You will hear each statement or question twice.

a. Me llamo ... **1.** ________

b. Muy bien, gracias. **2.** ________

c. Regular. **3.** ________

d. Mucho gusto. **4.** ________

e. Igualmente. **5.** ________

f. Hasta mañana. **6.** ________

Actividad 2

You have lost your dog, so you put up signs in your neighborhood asking your neighbors to call you if they see him. You will hear six messages on your answering machine from neighbors who have seen your dog. You will not understand everything they say, but listen carefully to find out their house number and what time they called so that you can track down your dog. Write down each house number and time on the chart. You will hear each message twice.

	NÚMERO DE CASA (*House number*)	HORA DE LA LLAMADA (*Time of call*)
1.	________	________
2.	________	________
3.	________	________
4.	________	________
5.	________	________
6.	________	________

Realidades A | Nombre ______ | Hora ______

Para empezar | Fecha ______ | AUDIO

Actividad 3

A new student has come into your Spanish class. He seems lost when the teacher asks the students to take out certain items. As you listen to what the teacher says, help him by identifying the picture that matches the item the teacher is asking the students to get out for class. You will hear each command twice.

Modelo ___f___ **1.** ______ **2.** ______ **3.** ______ **4.** ______ **5.** ______

a. b. c.

d. e. f.

Actividad 4

Your teacher is using a map and an alphabet/number grid to plan a class trip to Spain. The five dots on the grid represent cities in Spain where your group will stop. Listen as you hear the first letter/number combination, as in the game of Bingo. Find that dot on the grid and label it "1." Next to it, write the name of the city. After you hear the second letter/number combination, find the second dot and label it "2," writing the name of the city next to it, and so on for the rest of the dots. Connect the dots to show the route of the class trip. You will hear each phrase twice.

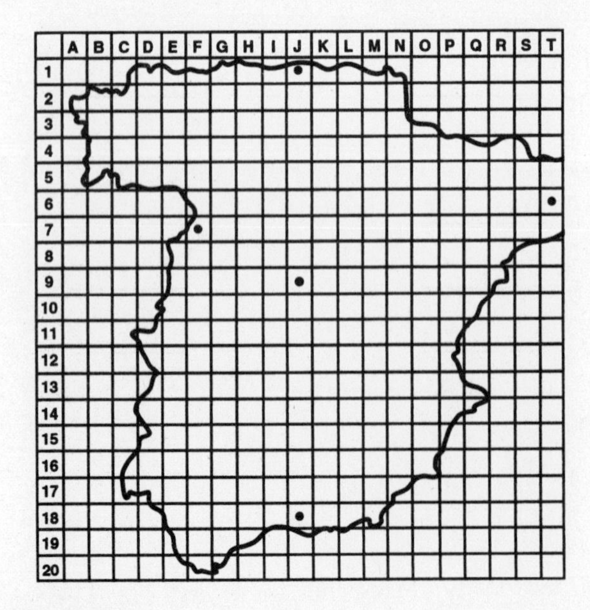

Nombre ____________ Hora ____________

Fecha ____________ AUDIO

Actividad 5

While on vacation in Uruguay, your teacher visits an elementary school classroom. Each student in the class tells your teacher his or her birthday (**cumpleaños**) and what the weather is like at that time of the year in Uruguay. Remember, in South America the seasons are the reverse of those in the United States. In the first column write out each student's date of birth, and in the second column what season his or her birthday is in. You will hear each sentence twice.

	DATE OF BIRTH	SEASON
1. Juan	____________	____________
2. María	____________	____________
3. Miguel	____________	____________
4. Óscar	____________	____________
5. Carolina	____________	____________
6. Marta	____________	____________
7. Elena	____________	____________
8. Pedro	____________	____________

Realidades A

Para empezar

Nombre ______ Hora ______

Fecha ______

WRITING

Actividad 6

Describe the monster below, telling how many of each body part he has (**El monstruo tiene ...**). Each blank corresponds to one letter. Each letter corresponds to a number, which appears underneath the blank. Use these numbers to figure out which sentence refers to which body part. The first one has been done for you.

Modelo El monstruo tiene D O S (9 15 20) C A B E Z A S (2 10 19 1 3 10 20).

1. El monstruo tiene ___ ___ ___ ___ (15 2 8 15) ___ ___ ___ ___ (15 17 15 20).
2. El monstruo tiene ___ ___ ___ (6 22 10) ___ ___ ___ ___ ___ (22 10 4 5 3) en cada cabeza.
3. El monstruo tiene ___ ___ ___ (6 22 10) ___ ___ ___ ___ (19 15 2 10) en cada cabeza.
4. El monstruo tiene ___ ___ ___ ___ ___ ___ (2 6 10 11 4 15) ___ ___ ___ ___ ___ ___ (19 4 10 3 15 20).
5. El monstruo tiene ___ ___ ___ ___ (11 4 1 20) ___ ___ ___ ___ ___ (9 1 9 15 20) en cada mano.
6. El monstruo tiene ___ ___ ___ ___ (20 1 5 20) ___ ___ ___ ___ ___ ___ ___ (16 5 1 4 22 10 20).

Nombre ____________________ Hora ____________

Fecha ____________________ **WRITING**

Actividad 7

A. It is September and school is finally in session. You already have some important dates to mark on the calendar. To make sure you have the right day, write the day of the week that each date falls on.

SEPTIEMBRE						
lunes	**martes**	**miércoles**	**jueves**	**viernes**	**sábado**	**domingo**
		1	2	3	4	5
6	7	8	9	10	11	12
13	14	15	16	17	18	19
20	21	22	23	24	25	26
27	28	29	30			

1. el tres de septiembre ____________________
2. el veinte de septiembre ____________________
3. el primero de septiembre ____________________
4. el veinticuatro de septiembre ____________________
5. el doce de septiembre ____________________
6. el dieciocho de septiembre ____________________
7. el siete de septiembre ____________________

B. Now, write in what month the following holidays occur.

1. el Día de San Valentín ____________________
2. el Día de San Patricio ____________________
3. la Navidad ____________________
4. el Año Nuevo ____________________
5. el Día de la Independencia ____________________

Actividad 8

Answer the questions below according to the map.

1. ¿Qué tiempo hace en el norte de México?

___

2. ¿Hace buen tiempo en el sur?

___

3. ¿Qué tiempo hace en el centro de México?

___

4. ¿Hace frío o calor en el este?

___

5. ¿Qué tiempo hace en el oeste?

___

6. ¿Qué estación es, probablemente?

___

Realidades A

Capítulo 1A

Nombre ______ Hora ______

Fecha ______

VIDEO

Introducción

Actividad 1

Do you like the video so far? Did you enjoy meeting the characters? Are you curious to find out more about their home cities? Look at the map below. Then, write the names of the video friends that live at each location. As you are doing this exercise, begin to familiarize yourself with the names of these locations: Madrid, España; Ciudad de México, México; San José, Costa Rica; San Antonio, Texas.

Esteban y Angélica	Ignacio y Ana	Claudia y Teresa	Raúl y Gloria

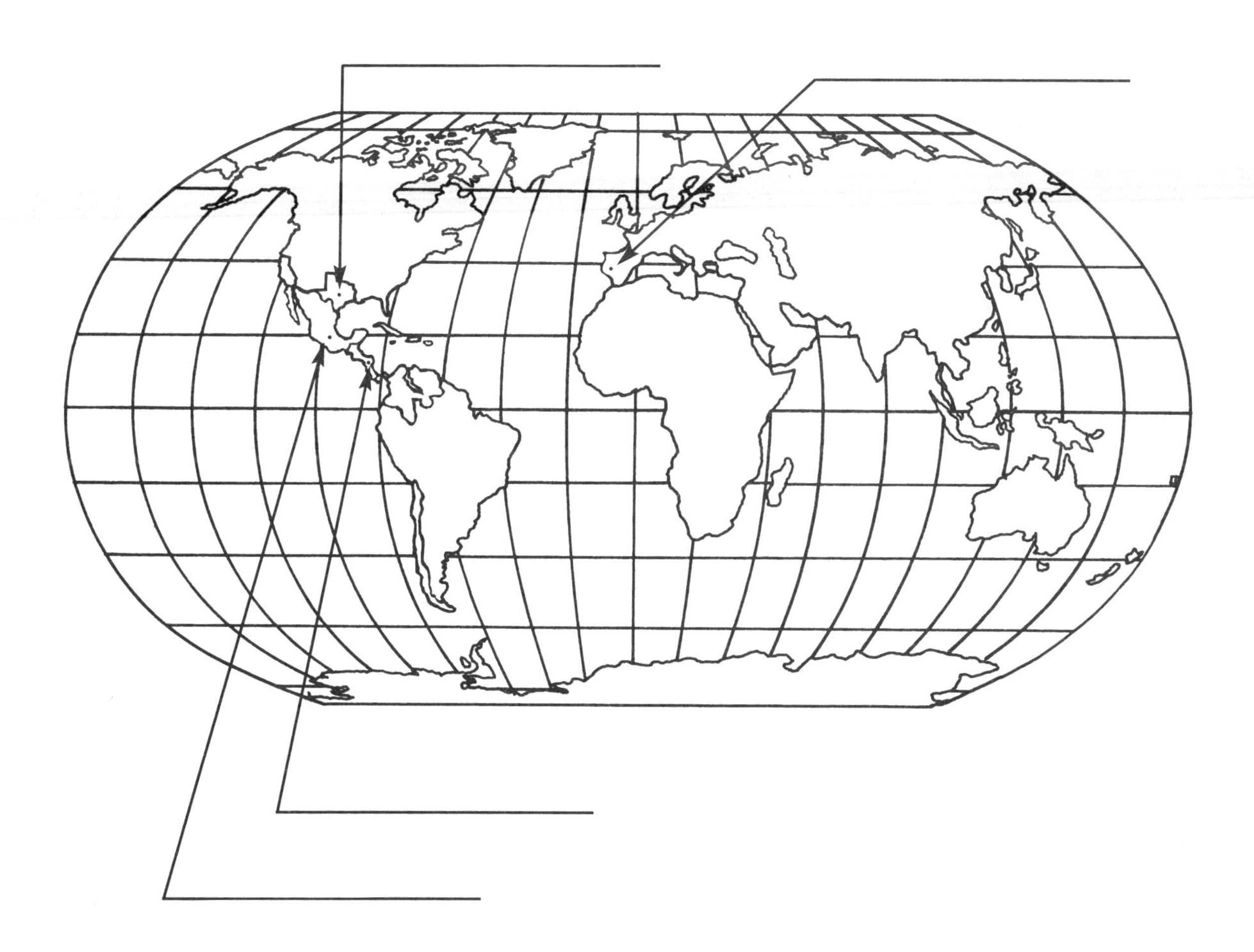

Realidades A | Nombre ____________ | Hora ____________

Capítulo 1A | Fecha ____________ | VIDEO

¿Comprendes?

Actividad 2

Match the characters with the activities they like to do or do not like to do.

1. Me llamo Ignacio y tengo 17 años. _____

2. Yo me llamo Ana y tengo 15 años. _____

3. Me llamo Claudia y tengo 16 años. _____

4. Y yo soy Teresa. Tengo 15 años. _____

5. Soy Esteban. Tengo 15 años. _____

6. Yo me llamo Angélica y tengo 16 años. _____

7. Soy Raúl y tengo 15 años. _____

8. Me llamo Gloria y tengo 14 años. _____

a. Me gusta escuchar música también. Pero me gusta más hablar por teléfono.

b. Me gusta usar la computadora.

c. A mí me gusta tocar la guitarra.

d. Me gusta practicar deportes, correr y montar en bicicleta.

e. Me gusta leer libros y revistas.

f. A mí me gusta ir a la escuela.

g. Me gusta más jugar videojuegos.

h. A mí no me gusta ni correr ni montar en bicicleta. A mí me gusta patinar.

Nombre ______ Hora ______

Fecha ______ VIDEO

Actividad 3

Decide whether response a, b, or c best describes the characters in each question.

1. When they are outside, what does Ana ask Ignacio? ____
   a. ¿Te gusta hablar por teléfono?
   b. ¿Qué te gusta hacer?
   c. ¿Te gusta tocar la guitarra?

2. Claudia and Teresa live in Mexico. What do they both like to do? ____
   a. pasar tiempo con amigos
   b. jugar videojuegos
   c. usar la computadora

3. What sports do Esteban and Angélica talk about? ____
   a. correr, montar en bicicleta y patinar
   b. esquiar, correr y nadar
   c. jugar al básquetbol, jugar al fútbol y montar en bicicleta

4. Does Raúl like to go to school? ____
   a. Sí. A Raúl le gusta mucho ir a la escuela.
   b. No. No le gusta nada.
   c. Pues… más o menos.

Y, ¿qué más?

Actividad 4

You have just seen and heard what these eight video friends like or do not like to do. Now fill in the blanks below to tell about things that you like to do and do not like to do.

1. Me gusta ______.
2. A mí me gusta más ______.
3. A mí no me gusta ______.
4. A mí no me gusta ni ______.

Nombre ______________________ Hora ______

Fecha ______________________ AUDIO

Actividad 5

You can learn a lot about a person from what he or she likes to do. You will hear two people from each group of three describe themselves. Listen and match the descriptions to the appropriate pictures. Put an *A* underneath the first person described, and a *B* underneath the second person described. You will hear each set of statements twice.

1. Luisa ______ Marta ______ Carmen ______

2. Marco ______ Javier ______ Alejandro ______

3. Mercedes ______ Ana ______ María ______

4. Carlos ______ Jaime ______ Luis ______

5. Isabel ______ Margarita ______ Cristina ______

Realidades A | Nombre ____ | Hora ____

Capítulo 1A | Fecha ____ | **AUDIO**

Actividad 6

A group of students from Peru will visit your school. Since your class will be hosting the students, your teacher is trying to match each of you with a visiting student who likes to do the same things as you do. Listen to the questions and write the students' answers in the blanks. Then, write which of the activities you like better. Find out if the student has the same preferences as you do. Follow the model. You will hear each conversation twice.

Modelo Guillermo: *cantar*

A mí: *Me gusta más bailar*.

1. Paco: ____

   A mí: ____.

2. Ana María: ____

   A mí: ____.

3. José Luis: ____

   A mí: ____.

4. Maricarmen: ____

   A mí: ____.

5. Luisa: ____

   A mí: ____.

Actividad 7

As one of the judges at your school's fall carnival, your job is to mark on the master tic tac toe board the progress of a live tic-tac-toe competition between Team X and Team O.

As each contestant comes to the microphone, you will hear "por X" or "por O" to indicate for which team he or she is playing. The contestant has to answer a question about activities in order to claim the square. Listen for the activity mentioned in each question, and put either an *X* or an *O* in the box under the picture of that activity.

At the end of this game round, see which team won! You will hear each statement twice.

Who won the game? ______________________________

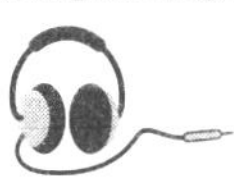

Actividad 8

Luisa, the host of your school's radio station talk show, is interviewing four new students. As you listen to the interview, write down one thing that each student likes to do, and one thing that each student does not like to do. You will hear the entire question and answer session repeated. You will hear this conversation twice.

	Armando	Josefina	Carlos	Marta
Likes				
Dislikes				

Actividad 9

As you turn on the radio, you hear a Spanish radio D.J. talking about the "Top Ten Tips" for being happy during this school year. As you listen, match the suggestion to one of the pictures and number them in the order the suggestions were given on the air. Remember to listen for cognates!

a. # ____	b. # ____	c. # ____	d. # ____	e. # ____
f. # ____	g. # ____	h. # ____	i. # ____	j. # ____

Realidades A

Nombre ______ Hora ______

Capítulo 1A

Fecha ______

WRITING

Actividad 10

Students like to do all sorts of activities during their free periods. Look at the picture below and write what each student is saying he or she likes to do. Then say whether or not you like to do those things. Follow the model.

Modelo EL PROFESOR: *A mí me gusta trabajar.*

TÚ: *A mí me gusta trabajar también.*

ESTUDIANTE #1: ______

TÚ: ______

ESTUDIANTE #2: ______

TÚ: ______

ESTUDIANTE #3: ______

TÚ: ______

ESTUDIANTE #4: ______

TÚ: ______

ESTUDIANTE #5: ______

TÚ: ______

ESTUDIANTE #6: ______

TÚ: ______

Nombre ______ Hora ______

Fecha ______

WRITING

Actividad 11

It is your first day at your new school, and your new friend Elena is interviewing you for the school newspaper. In the spaces provided, write your answers to the questions that Elena asks you.

ELENA: —Buenos días. ¿Cómo estás?

TÚ: —______

ELENA: —¿Qué te gusta hacer?

TÚ: —______

ELENA: —¿Te gusta ir a la escuela?

TÚ: —______

ELENA: —¿Qué te gusta hacer en casa?

TÚ: —______

ELENA: —¿Te gusta escribir o leer cuentos?

TÚ: —______

ELENA: —¿Qué más te gusta hacer?

TÚ: —______

ELENA: —Pues, muchas gracias por la entrevista. Buena suerte.

TÚ: —______

Realidades A | Nombre ______ Hora ______

Capítulo 1A | Fecha ______ **WRITING**

Actividad 12

A. Your classmates have signed up for different clubs. Look at the flyers below to see who signed up for which club. Then, decide how each student might answer the questions below based on the club that each one signed up for.

El Club Educativo
El club ideal para estudiantes a quienes les gusta ir a la escuela.
Actividades:
- usar la computadora
- leer y escribir cuentos
- estudiar

Eduardo ______
Eugenia ______
Esteban ______

El Club Deportista
El club ideal para estudiantes a quienes les gusta practicar deportes.
Actividades:
- nadar
- correr
- practicar deportes

Diana ______
Dolores ______
Diego ______

EL CLUB MUSICAL
El club ideal para estudiantes a quienes les gusta la música.
ACTIVIDADES:
- TOCAR EL PIANO O LA GUITARRA
- CANTAR
- BAILAR

MARICARMEN ______
MANOLO ______
MÓNICA ______

Modelo Eduardo, ¿te gusta tocar la guitarra?

No, no me gusta tocar la guitarra. Me gusta estudiar.

1. Diana, ¿te gusta leer o escribir cuentos?
______
2. Manolo, ¿qué te gusta hacer?
______
3. Diego, ¿te gusta ir a la escuela para usar la computadora?
______
4. Mónica, ¿te gusta nadar o correr?
______
5. Eugenia, ¿qué te gusta hacer?
______

B. Now, pick which club you would join and say why. Follow the model.

Modelo *Prefiero el Club Educativo porque me gusta ir a la escuela.*

Prefiero el Club ______ porque ______
______

Nombre ______ Hora ______

Fecha ______

WRITING

Actividad 13

A. Write two sentences about things that you like to do, and two sentences about things that you do not like to do. Follow the model.

Modelo *A mí me gusta leer.*

No me gusta correr.

1. ______
2. ______
3. ______
4. ______

B. Now, use your sentences from Part A to write a letter to your new penpal that will tell her a little bit about you.

29/9/2003

Saludos,

______

También ______

Un abrazo,

______

Antes de ver el video

Actividad 1

During the video, Teresa, Claudia, Pedro, and Esteban describe each other in e-mails. How would you describe yourself? Below is a list of descriptive words. Check off the words that describe you.

Soy...

- ❑ artístico, -a
- ❑ atrevido, -a
- ❑ deportista
- ❑ desordenado, -a
- ❑ estudioso, -a
- ❑ gracioso, -a
- ❑ impaciente
- ❑ inteligente
- ❑ ordenado, -a
- ❑ paciente
- ❑ reservado, -a
- ❑ serio, -a
- ❑ simpático, -a
- ❑ sociable
- ❑ talentoso, -a
- ❑ trabajador, -ora

¿Comprendes?

Actividad 2

Fill in the blanks with the appropriate word or phrase from the bank. You may have to watch the video several times to remember each character well.

misteriosa	reservado	ordenados	inteligente
serio	trabajadora	sociable	
simpática	hablar por teléfono	buena	

1. A Pedro no le gusta ni bailar ni cantar. Es ____________________.

Pero él escribe: "Soy muy gracioso. No soy muy ____________________."

Nombre ____________________ Hora ____________

Fecha ____________________

VIDEO

2. Teresa, desde un cibercafé en la Ciudad de México, escribe: "Yo soy *Chica* ____________________."

3. Ella es la ____________________ amiga de Claudia.

4. Le gusta ____________________, pero no le gusta ir a la escuela.

5. En la computadora, Claudia se llama *Chica* ____________________.

6. A ella le gusta la escuela; es muy ____________________, estudiosa y ____________________.

7. También le gustan los chicos inteligentes y ____________________.

8. A Pedro le gusta *Chica misteriosa*. Ella también es una chica ____________________.

Actividad 3

According to Esteban, Pedro is quiet and reserved. Yet, in his e-mail, he writes the opposite. Read what he writes about himself in his e-mail. Then, write what he is really like by filling in the blanks.

```
Me llamo Chico sociable. ¡Qué coincidencia! Me gusta
pasar tiempo con mis amigos... Me gusta escuchar
música. Según mis amigos soy muy gracioso. No soy muy
serio.  Escríbeme.
```

1. *Chico sociable,* el ________________ de Esteban, se llama ________________.
2. Según Esteban, él no es un chico ________________. Él es ________________.
3. A Pedro no le gusta ni ________________ ni ________________.
4. Pedro no es muy ________________. Él es muy ________________.

Y, ¿qué más?

Actividad 4

Describe people you know using each of the adjectives from the following list. Follow the model.

paciente	inteligente	sociable	impaciente	deportista

Modelo *La profesora de español es muy inteligente.*

____

____

____

____

Nombre _______________ Hora _______________

Fecha _______________

AUDIO

Actividad 5

You are a volunteer for a service at your school that helps new students meet other new students in order to make the transition easier. People who are interested in participating in this program have left messages describing themselves. Listen as the students describe themselves, and put a check mark in at least two columns that match what each student says. Then write the names of the most well-matched students. You will hear each statement twice.

BUENOS AMIGOS

	CARMEN	PABLO	ANA	ANDRÉS	RAQUEL	JORGE
serio(a)						
reservado(a)						
deportista						
estudioso(a)						
talentoso(a)						
gracioso(a)						
atrevido(a)						
trabajador(a)						
artístico(a)						
sociable						
romántico(a)						

BUENOS AMIGOS:

1. _______________ y _______________
2. _______________ y _______________
3. _______________ y _______________

Nombre ____________________ Hora __________

Fecha ____________________

AUDIO

Actividad 6

What is your favorite season of the year? Your choice could say a lot about you. Listen as talk-show psychologist Doctor Armando describes people according to their preferred season (**estación preferida**) of the year. What characteristics go with each season? Listen and put a check mark in the appropriate boxes. By the way, is it true what he says about you and your favorite season? You will hear each statement twice.

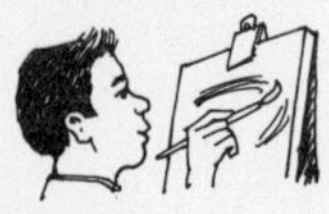				

Mi estación preferida es ____________________. Según el Dr. Armando, yo soy

____.

Actividad 7

Your Spanish teacher encourages you to speak Spanish outside of class. As you walk down the hall, you hear parts of your classmates' conversations in Spanish. Listen to the conversations and decide whether they are talking about a boy, a girl, or if you can't tell by what is being said. Place a check mark in the appropriate box of the table. You will hear each statement twice.

	#1	#2	#3	#4	#5	#6	#7	#8
(boy)								
(girl)								
?								

Actividad 8

Listen as Nacho describes his ex-girlfriend. How many things do they have in common? Put an *X* on the pictures that show ways in which they are very different and put a circle around the pictures that show ways they are very similar. You will hear each set of statements twice.

1. 

2. 

3. 

4. 

5. 

Nombre _______________ Hora _______________

Fecha _______________

AUDIO

Actividad 9

Some people say we are what we dream! Listen as Antonieta calls in and describes her dream (**sueño**) to Doctor Armando, the radio talk show psychologist. Draw a circle around the pictures below that match what she dreams about herself.

After you hear Antonieta's call, tell a partner what kinds of things would be in a dream that reveals what you like to do and what kind of person you are. You might begin with "**En mi sueño, me gusta...**". You will hear this dialogue twice.

Realidades **A** Nombre ________________ Hora ________

Capítulo 1B Fecha ________________ **WRITING**

Actividad 10

A. Fill in the words using the art as clues.

1. Marta es una chica ______________.

2. Cristina es mi amiga ______________.

3. Alicia es muy ______________.

4. Isa es una chica ______________.

5. Alejandro es muy ______________.

6. Carlos es un chico ______________.

7. Kiko es ______________.

8. Pepe es mi amigo ______________.

B. Now, check your answers by finding them in the word search.

N E P M V P I Q U U T D
T R A B A J A D O R A E
A S O I D U T S E D G S
L A K U X M A L E A R O
E M D I C Z P P O C A R
N T P A O X O J Z I C D
T I U M N R U F R T I E
O Q K I T E I T E S O N
S M X I E T D G P I S A
A O S L U R M R Y T O D
P T L A E U U J O R H O
A S O C I A B L E A E T

Nombre ______________________ Hora ______________

Fecha ______________________ WRITING

Actividad 11

Frida and Diego, who are opposites, are talking on the phone. Frida, the sociable one, is doing all the talking. Using the pictures of the friends below, write what Frida might be saying about herself and about Diego. Follow the models.

Modelo *Yo soy deportista.*

1. ______________________
2. ______________________
3. ______________________
4. ______________________
5. ______________________

Modelo *Tú eres paciente.*

1. ______________________
2. ______________________
3. ______________________
4. ______________________
5. ______________________

Realidades 

Capítulo 1B

Nombre _______________ Hora _______________

Fecha _______________ **WRITING**

Actividad 12

Answer the following questions. Be sure to use the definite or indefinite article where appropriate. Follow the model.

Modelo ¿Cómo es tu mamá (*mother*)?

Ella es simpática y graciosa.

1. ¿Cómo eres tú?

____

2. ¿Cómo es tu profesor(a) de español?

____

3. ¿Cómo es tu mejor amigo(a)?

____

4. ¿Cómo es el presidente?

____

5. ¿Cómo es el director/la directora (*principal*) de tu escuela?

____

6. ¿Qué te duele?

____

7. ¿Cuál es la fecha de hoy?

____

8. ¿Cuál es la fecha del Día de la Independencia?

____

9. ¿Cuál es tu estación favorita?

____

10. ¿Qué hora es?

____

Nombre ______ Hora ______

Fecha ______ **WRITING**

Actividad 13

A reporter for the school newspaper has asked you and several other students in your classroom to submit an article for the paper. The article is about personality traits and activities people like and dislike.

A. Think about your own personality traits. Write four adjectives that describe what you are like and four that describe what you are not like.

SOY	NO SOY

B. Now, write four things that you like to do and four things that you do not like to do.

ME GUSTA	NO ME GUSTA

C. Now, write your article using the information you have compiled about yourself.

Realidades A — Nombre ____ Hora ____

Capítulo 2A — Fecha ____ VIDEO

Antes de ver el video

Actividad 1

Think of two of your favorite and two of your least favorite classes. Write the name of each class, when you have it, and why it is your favorite or least favorite.

Clase	Hora	Comentarios

¿Comprendes?

Actividad 2

Claudia had a bad day. Circle the correct answer to explain what happened to her.

1. Claudia tiene un día difícil en el colegio (*high school*). ¿Por qué?
   a. A Claudia no le gusta su colegio.
   b. Claudia no tiene amigos.
   c. Tiene problemas con el horario.
   d. A Claudia no le gustan las matemáticas.
2. ¿En qué hora tiene Claudia la clase de matemáticas?
   a. en la primera hora c. en la quinta hora
   b. en la tercera hora d. todas las anteriores (*all of the above*)
3. Claudia habla con la persona que hace el horario. ¿Cómo se llama?
   a. Sra. Santoro b. Sr. López c. Srta. García d. Sr. Treviño
4. Para Teresa la clase de inglés es
   a. aburrida. b. interesante. c. fantástica. d. difícil.
5. En la tercera hora Claudia piensa que las matemáticas son aburridas, porque
   a. es el primer día de clases. c. tiene seis clases de matemáticas hoy.
   b. la profesora es muy divertida. d. no entiende las matemáticas.

Actividad 3

Write **cierto** (*true*) or **falso** (*false*) next to each statement.

1. La clase de matemáticas es muy fácil para Claudia. ________
2. Teresa habla con el Sr. Treviño del problema con su horario. ________
3. Teresa y Claudia tienen el almuerzo a la misma hora. ________
4. Teresa tiene la clase de ciencias sociales en la tercera hora. ________

Y, ¿qué más?

Actividad 4

Complete the paragraph with information about your teachers, classes, school, and friends.

El profesor / La profesora que más me gusta es el Sr. / la Sra. ________________.

Él / Ella enseña la clase de ________________ en la ________________ hora y su clase es muy ________________.

Después de la ________________ hora tengo el almuerzo. Me gusta mucho porque puedo estar con ________________ y ________________; ellos / ellas son mis amigos / amigas.

El director / La directora de mi colegio se llama ________________. Él / Ella es muy ________________ y ________________.

Nombre ______ Hora ______

Fecha ______

AUDIO

Actividad 5

You overhear several people in the hall trying to find out if they have classes together this year. As you listen to each conversation, write an *X* in the box under ***SÍ*** if they have a class together, or under ***NO*** if they do not. You will hear each conversation twice.

	SÍ	NO
1.	______	______
2.	______	______
3.	______	______
4.	______	______
5.	______	______

Actividad 6

As you stand outside the school counselor's office, you hear four students trying to talk to him. They are all requesting to get out of a certain class. From the part of the conversation that you hear, write in the blank the class from which each student is requesting a transfer. You will hear each statement twice.

CLASE	PROFESOR(A)
1. matemáticas	el profesor Pérez
2. arte	la profesora Muñoz
3. español	el profesor Cortez
4. ciencias sociales	la profesora Lenis
5. almuerzo	
6. ciencias	el profesor Gala
7. educación física	el profesor Fernández
8. inglés	la profesora Ochoa

1. La clase de ______
2. La clase de ______
3. La clase de ______
4. La clase de ______

Actividad 7

Emilio, a new student from Bolivia, is attending his first pep assembly! He is eager to make friends and begins talking to Diana, who is sitting next to him. Listen to their conversation. If they have something in common, place a check mark in the column labeled **Ellos**. If the statement only applies to Emilio, place a check mark in the column labeled **Él**. If the statement only applies to Diana, place a check mark in the column labeled **Ella**. **Note:** Be sure you have placed a check mark in ONLY one of the columns for each statement. You will hear the conversation twice.

INFORMACIÓN	ÉL	ELLA	ELLOS
Tiene la clase de español en la primera hora.			
Tiene la clase de español en la segunda hora.			
Tiene una profesora simpática.			
Tiene una profesora graciosa.			
Tiene una clase de arte en la quinta hora.			
Tiene una clase de educación física en la quinta hora.			
Practica deportes.			
Estudia mucho en la clase de matemáticas.			
Es trabajador(a).			
Tiene mucha tarea.			
Tiene almuerzo a las once y media.			

Nombre ______ Hora ______

Fecha ______

AUDIO

Actividad 8

Listen as four people talk about what they do during the day. There will be some things that all four people do and other things that not all of them do. Fill in the grid with a check mark if the person says he or she does a certain activity. Also, fill in the **Yo** column with a check mark for the activities that you do every day. You will hear each set of statements twice.

	EVA	DAVID	RAQUEL	JOSÉ	YO

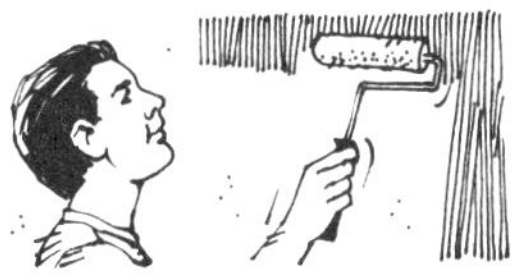					

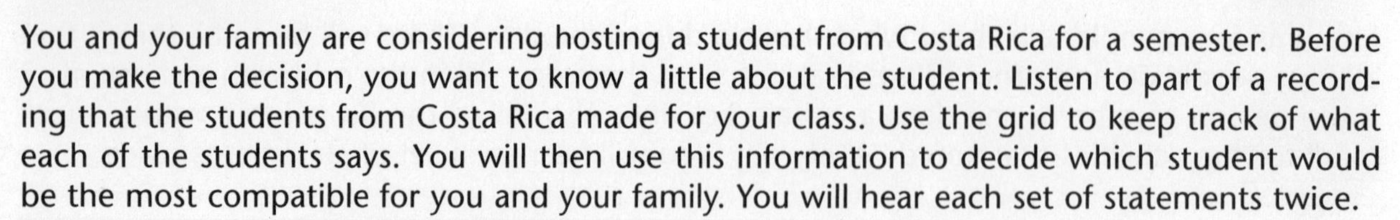

Realidades A | Nombre ______ | Hora ______

Capítulo 2A | Fecha ______ | AUDIO

Actividad 9

You and your family are considering hosting a student from Costa Rica for a semester. Before you make the decision, you want to know a little about the student. Listen to part of a recording that the students from Costa Rica made for your class. Use the grid to keep track of what each of the students says. You will then use this information to decide which student would be the most compatible for you and your family. You will hear each set of statements twice.

Estudiante	Característica(s) de la personalidad	Clase favorita	Actividades favoritas
JORGE			
LUZ			
MARCO			
CRISTINA			

Which student is most like you? ______________________________

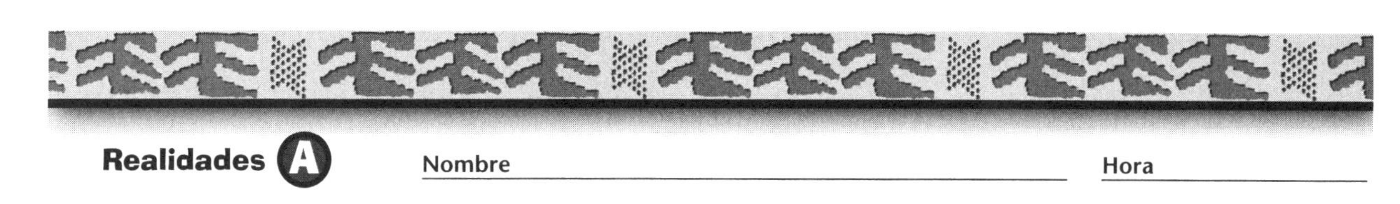

Realidades A

Nombre ______ Hora ______

Capítulo 2A

Fecha ______

WRITING

Actividad 10

Your classmates are curious about your schedule at school. Using complete sentences, tell them what classes you have during the day. Follow the model.

Modelo *Yo tengo la clase de inglés en la segunda hora.*

1. ______
2. ______
3. ______
4. ______
5. ______
6. ______
7. ______

Actividad 11

Answer the following questions using the subject pronoun suggested by the pictures. Follow the model.

Modelo 

¿Quiénes usan la computadora?

Ellos usan la computadora.

1. 

¿Quién habla con Teresa?

______.

2. 

¿Quién habla con Paco?

______.

Nombre ______________________ Hora __________

Fecha ______________________ **WRITING**

3. ¿Quiénes hablan?

____.

4. ¿Cómo es el Sr. García?

____.

5. Ana, ¿tienes la clase de arte en la primera hora?

Sí, ____.

Ana

6. ¿Cristina y yo somos muy buenas amigas?

Sí, ____.

Cristina Yo

Realidades A

Capítulo 2A

Nombre ______ Hora ______

Fecha ______ WRITING

Actividad 12

A new student at your school has come to you for information about how things work at your school and what your day is like. Answer the student's questions truthfully in complete sentences. Follow the model.

Modelo ¿La secretaria habla mucho por teléfono?

Sí, ella habla mucho ______.

1. ¿Estudias inglés en la primera hora?

   ______.

2. ¿Quién enseña la clase de matemáticas?

   ______.

3. ¿Necesito un diccionario para la clase de arte?

   ______.

4. ¿Cantas en el coro (*choir*)?

   ______.

5. ¿Pasas mucho tiempo en la cafetería?

   ______.

6. ¿Uds. practican deportes en la clase de educación física?

   ______.

7. ¿Los estudiantes usan las computadoras en la clase de ciencias naturales?

   ______.

8. ¿Uds. bailan en la clase de español?

   ______.

9. ¿Los profesores tocan el piano en la clase de música?

   ______.

10. ¿Los estudiantes hablan mucho en la clase de francés?

    ______

Actividad 13

A. List two classes that you have, when you have them, and who the teacher is.

	Clase	Hora	Profesor(a)
1.			
2.			

B. Now, write complete sentences about whether or not you like each class from Part A. Make sure to tell why you do or do not like each class.

Clase 1:

Clase 2:

C. Now, using the information from Parts A and B, write a paragraph about one of the classes. Make sure to tell the name of the class, when you have it, and who the teacher is. You should also describe your teacher, tell what you do in class, and say whether or not you like the class.

Realidades A

Capítulo 2B

Nombre ______ Hora ______

Fecha ______

VIDEO

Antes de ver el video

Actividad 1

Look around your classroom and make a list of five items that you see. Then, describe their location. Follow the model.

	COSA	DÓNDE ESTÁ
Modelo	*la papelera*	*debajo del reloj*
1.		
2.		
3.		
4.		
5.		

¿Comprendes?

Actividad 2

Using the screen grabs as clues, answer the following questions with the correct information from the video.

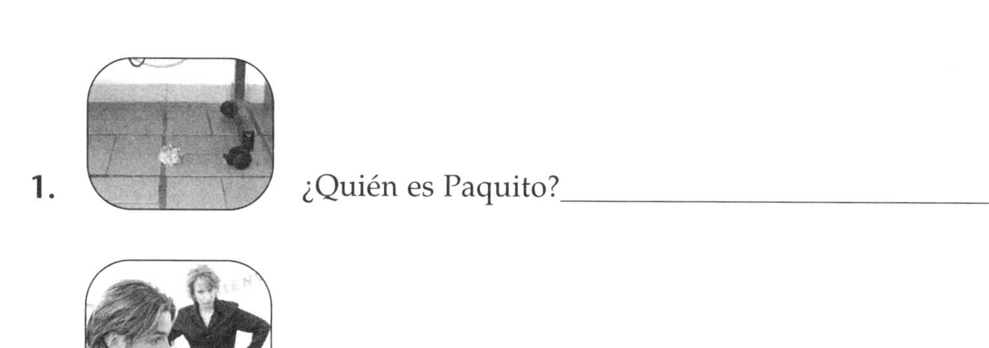

1. ¿Quién es Paquito? ______

2. ¿Qué le pasa a Manolo? Él no tiene ______.

3. ¿Quién tiene el hámster? ______

4. Los estudiantes están en ______________________.

5. ¿Para qué es el hámster? Es para ______________________.

Actividad 3

Next to each phrase, write the name of the character who said it in the video.

1. "¿Un ratón en la clase de ciencias sociales? ¡Imposible!" ______________
2. "¡No es un ratón! Es mi hámster." ______________
3. "Señorita, necesito hablar con usted más tarde." ______________
4. "Carlos, no tengo mi tarea." ______________
5. "¡Aquí está! Está en mi mochila." ______________
6. "Paquito, mi precioso. Ven aquí. ¿Estás bien?" ______________

Y, ¿qué más?

Actividad 4

Imagine that Paquito is running around in your classroom. Using the prepositions that you have just learned, indicate four places where he might be. Follow the example below.

Modelo *Paquito está encima de la mochila.*

1. ______________________________
2. ______________________________
3. ______________________________
4. ______________________________

Realidades A | Nombre | Hora

Capítulo 2B | Fecha

AUDIO

Actividad 5

As you look at the picture, decide whether the statements you hear are **ciertos** or **falsos**. You will hear each statement twice.

1. cierto	falso	**6.** cierto	falso	**11.** cierto	falso
2. cierto	falso	**7.** cierto	falso	**12.** cierto	falso
3. cierto	falso	**8.** cierto	falso	**13.** cierto	falso
4. cierto	falso	**9.** cierto	falso	**14.** cierto	falso
5. cierto	falso	**10.** cierto	falso	**15.** cierto	falso

Nombre ______ Hora ______

Fecha ______ AUDIO

Actividad 6

Tomás suddenly realizes in the middle of his science class that the notebook with his entire class project in it is missing! He asks several people if they know where it is. Listen as different people tell Tomás where they think his notebook is. In the timeline, write what classroom he goes to and where in the classroom he looks, in the order in which you hear them. You will hear this conversation twice.

	Susana	Antonio	Noé	Sr. Atkins
Classroom				
Location in room				

Where did Tomás eventually find his notebook?______

Actividad 7

It's time to take the Spanish Club picture for the yearbook, but there are several people who have still not arrived. Andrés, the president, decides to use his cell phone to find out where people are. As you listen to the first part of each conversation, complete the sentences below with the information he finds out. For example, you might write:
Beto está en el gimnasio.
You will hear each dialogue twice.

1. Los dos profesores de español ______.
2. Javier ______.
3. Alejandra y Sara ______.
4. Mateo ______.
5. José y Antonieta ______.

Nombre ______ Hora ______

Fecha ______ **WRITING**

Actividad 10

After your first day of school, you are describing your classroom to your parents. Using the picture below, tell them how many of each object there are in the room. Follow the model.

Modelo *Hay un escritorio en la sala de clases.*

1. ______
2. ______
3. ______
4. ______
5. ______
6. ______
7. ______

Nombre ______ Hora ______

Fecha ______

WRITING

Actividad 11

You are describing your classroom to your Spanish-speaking pen pal. Using complete sentences and the verb **estar**, tell what is in your room and where each item is located. Follow the model.

Modelo *Hay una mesa en la clase. Está al lado de la puerta.*

1. ______
2. ______
3. ______
4. ______
5. ______
6. ______
7. ______
8. ______

Actividad 12

Answer the following questions about things you have for school. Use the pictures as a guide. Follow the model.

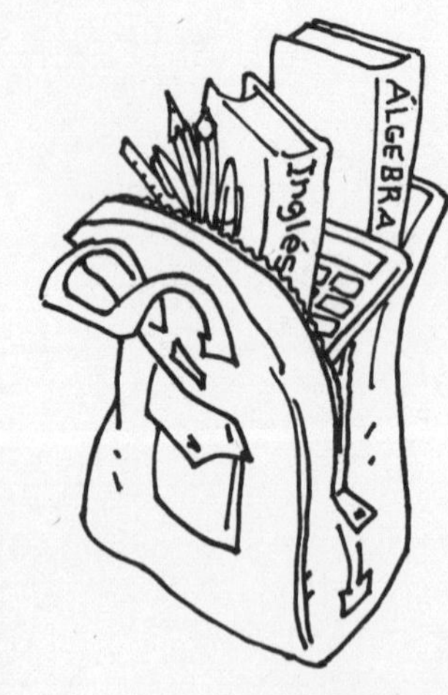

Modelo ¿Qué hay en la mochila?

En la mochila hay unos lápices y bolígrafos. También hay una calculadora y dos libros: el libro de matemáticas y el libro de inglés.

Realidades A

Capítulo 2B

Nombre ____________________ Hora ____________

Fecha ____________________

WRITING

1. ¿Qué hay en la clase de ciencias sociales?

____

____

____

____

____

2. ¿Qué hay encima del escritorio? ¿Y al lado? ¿Y detrás?

____

____

____

____

____

Realidades Ⓐ Nombre ____________________ Hora ____________

Capítulo 2B Fecha ____________________ **WRITING**

Actividad 13

The two rooms pictured below were once identical, but Sala 2 has been rearranged. Look at each picture carefully. Circle seven items in Sala 2 that are different from Sala 1. Then, write sentences about how Sala 2 is different. Follow the model.

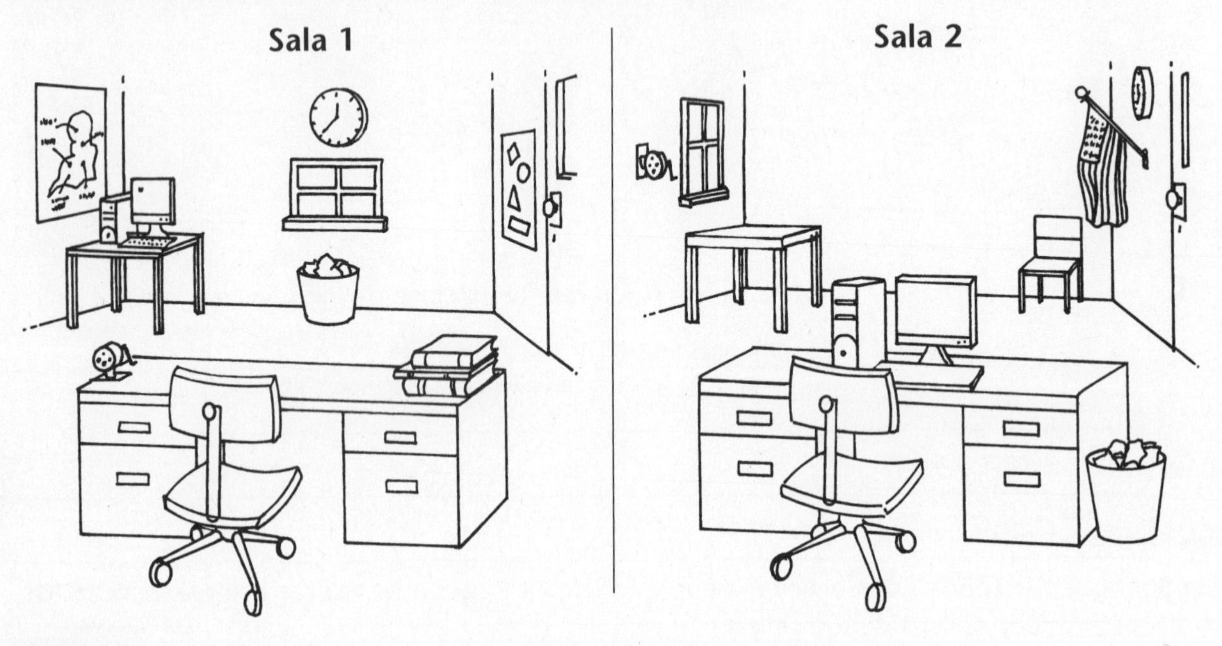

Modelo *En la sala 2 no hay libros encima del escritorio.*

1. ______________________________

2. ______________________________

3. ______________________________

4. ______________________________

5. ______________________________

6. ______________________________

7. ______________________________

Antes de ver el video

Actividad 1

What do you like to eat for breakfast and lunch? Fill in the chart with that information.

Desayuno	Almuerzo

¿Comprendes?

Actividad 2

Think about the foods Rosa believes people in the United States eat for breakfast. What do Tomás and Raúl really eat?

1. ¿Qué come Tomás para el desayuno?

Tomás bebe ______________ y come ______________ para el desayuno.

2. Y, ¿qué come Raúl?

Raúl bebe ______________ y ______________, come ______________, y a veces también come un ______________.

Nombre ______________________ Hora __________

Fecha ______________________

VIDEO

Actividad 3

Although Rosa makes a big breakfast for Tomás that day, the family does not eat very much regularly. Answer the questions below.

1. ¿Quién prepara el desayuno? ______________________

2. Lorenzo: "Es mucha comida, ¿no? ______________, ______________, ______________, ______________, ______________..." Rosa: "En los Estados Unidos, todos comen mucho en el desayuno."

3. Lorenzo: "Nosotros nunca comemos mucho en el desayuno, Rosa. Mira, yo sólo bebo un ______________ y a veces como un ______________."

4. Según Rosa, en los Estados Unidos comemos huevos, salchichas, tocino y pan tostado en el desayuno y ______________________ ______________________ en el almuerzo.

Y, ¿qué más?

Actividad 4

Do you recall what you wrote in **Actividad** 1 about foods that you like to eat? Now that you have heard people in Costa Rica talk about what they eat, write down three questions of your own to ask a classmate about food. With a partner, ask your questions and compare answers.

¿____?

¿____?

¿____?

Nombre ____________________ Hora ____________

Fecha ____________________ **AUDIO**

Actividad 5

You are helping out a friend at the counter of Restaurante El Gaucho in Argentina. Listen to the orders and record the quantity of each item ordered by each customer in the appropriate box of the chart. You will hear each conversation twice.

RESTAURANTE EL GAUCHO

El almuerzo	Cliente 1	Cliente 2	Cliente 3	Cliente 4
Ensalada				
Hamburguesa				
Hamburguesa con queso				
Sándwich de jamón y queso				
Perro caliente				
Pizza				
Papas fritas				
Refresco				
Té helado				
Galletas				

Nombre ______________________ Hora ______

Fecha ______________________ AUDIO

Actividad 6

While working at the Hotel Buena Vista, you need to record breakfast orders for room service. Use the grid to make your report. First, listen carefully for the room number and write it in the appropriate box. Then write in the time requested. Finally, put a check mark next to each item ordered by the person in that room. You will hear each set of statements twice.

HOTEL BUENA VISTA

Número de habitación (*room number*)					
Hora de servicio					
Jugo de naranja					
Jugo de manzana					
Cereal					
Pan tostado					
Huevos					
Jamón					
Tocino					
Salchichas					
Yogur de fresas					
Café					
Café con leche					
Té					

Nombre ______________________ Hora __________

Fecha ______________________ **AUDIO**

Actividad 7

You are waiting in line at a restaurant counter. You hear people behind you talking about your friends. Listen carefully so you can figure out whom they're talking about. Pay close attention to verb and adjective endings. Put a check mark in the column after each conversation. You will hear each set of statements twice.

	Carlos	Gabriela	Carlos y sus amigos	Gabriela y sus amigas
1.	______	______	______	______
2.	______	______	______	______
3.	______	______	______	______
4.	______	______	______	______
5.	______	______	______	______
6.	______	______	______	______
7.	______	______	______	______

Actividad 8

Listen as actors from a popular Spanish soap opera are interviewed on the radio program called **"Las dietas de los famosos"** (*Diets of the Famous*). As you listen, write **sí** if the person mentions that he or she eats or drinks something most days. Write **no** if the person says that he or she never eats or drinks the item. You will hear this conversation twice.

	Lana Lote	Óscar Oso	Pepe Pluma	Tita Trompo

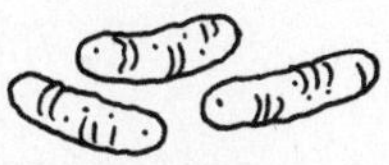				

Nombre ______ Hora ______

Fecha ______

AUDIO

	Lana Lote	Óscar Oso	Pepe Pluma	Tita Trompo
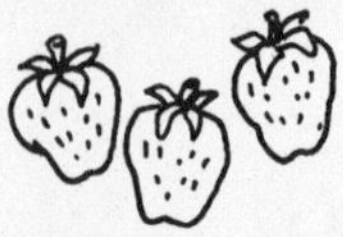				
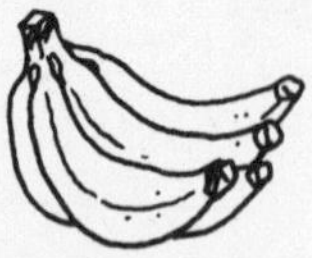				
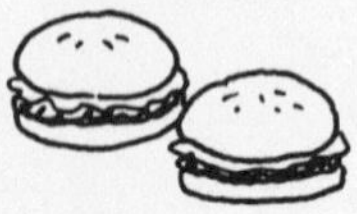				
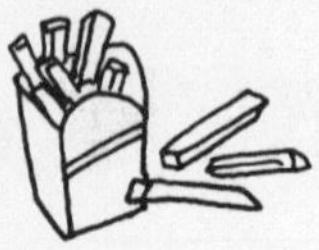				
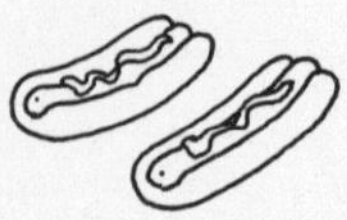				
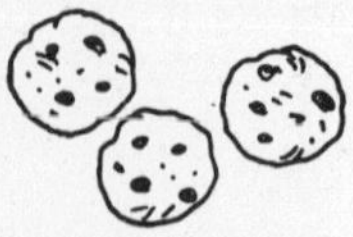				
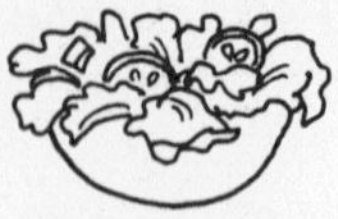				
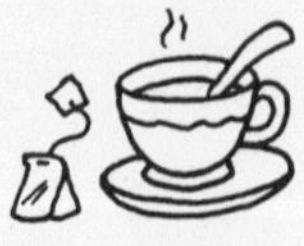				
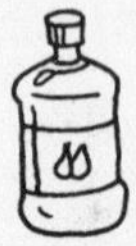				
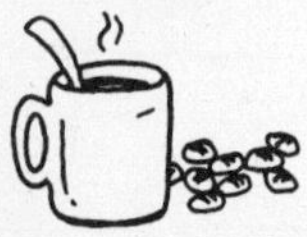				

Actividad 9

Listen as the woman at the table next to you tries to help a child order from the menu. As you listen, check off the items on the menu that the child says he likes and those he dislikes. Then in the space provided, write what you think would be an "acceptable" lunch for him. You will hear this conversation twice.

le gusta								
no le gusta								

Un almuerzo bueno para Beto es ____

____.

Nombre ______________________ Hora ______

Fecha ______________________

WRITING

Actividad 10

You have decided to help your parents by doing the food shopping for the week. Your friend Rodrigo is helping you make the shopping list. Complete the conversation below using the picture and your own food preferences.

RODRIGO: ¿Qué hay de beber?

TÚ: ____

RODRIGO: ¿Quieres (*do you want*) algo más?

TÚ: ____

____

RODRIGO: ¿Qué hay de comer para el desayuno?

TÚ: ____

RODRIGO: ¿Qué más quieres, entonces?

TÚ: ____

____

RODRIGO: ¿Qué hay para el almuerzo?

TÚ: ____

RODRIGO: ¿Y quieres algo más?

TÚ: ____

____

RODRIGO: ¿Y qué frutas necesitan?

TÚ : ____

Nombre _______________ Hora _______________

Fecha _______________ **WRITING**

Actividad 11

Describe each of the following scenes using as many **-er** and **-ir** verbs as you can. Use complete sentences.

____

____

____

____

yo | Ana y yo

tú | los estudiantes

____

____

____

____

Actividad 12

In anticipation of your arrival in Spain next week, your host sister writes to ask you about your favorite foods. Complete your response below with sentences using the verbs **gustar** and **encantar**.

Estimada Margarita:

Gracias por su carta. Hay muchas comidas que me gustan. Para el desayuno,

____. También

____. Pero no

____.

Pero me encanta más el almuerzo. Por ejemplo, ____________________

____. También

________________________. Pero no ____________________

____.

¿Y a ti? ¿Te gustan las hamburguesas? ¿ ______________________

______________________________? ¿______________

__________________________? ¿__________________

______________________________?

Nos vemos en una semana.

Un fuerte abrazo,

Melinda

Actividad 13

The school nurse is teaching a class on nutrition and asks everyone to fill out a survey about what he or she eats. Using complete sentences, write your responses below.

1. ¿Qué comes y bebes en el desayuno?

____

2. ¿Qué come y bebe tu familia en el almuerzo?

____

3. ¿Qué comida te encanta?

____

Antes de ver el video

Actividad 1

Think about the typical diet of a teenager. Which foods are healthy choices and which ones are not? Make a list of five foods in each category.

Comida buena para la salud ☺	Comida mala para la salud ☹
______	______
______	______
______	______
______	______
______	______

¿Comprendes?

Actividad 2

Write the name of the person from the video who made each statement.

1. "El café de aquí es muy bueno." ______
2. "No, no; un refresco no; un jugo de fruta." ______
3. "En Costa Rica, un refresco es un jugo de fruta." ______
4. "Yo hago mucho ejercicio..." ______
5. "Aquí en San José, todos caminamos mucho." ______
6. "... aquí una soda no es una bebida; es un restaurante." ______
7. "Me encanta el gallo pinto." ______

Realidades 

Nombre ______________________ Hora ____________

Capítulo 3B

Fecha ______________________

VIDEO

Actividad 3

Answer the questions.

1. 

¿Qué es muy importante para Costa Rica?

____

2. 

Según Raúl, ¿qué es bueno de Costa Rica?

____

3. 

Según Tomás, ¿qué es bueno para la salud?

____

4. 

¿Qué hacen todos en San José?

____

5. 

¿Qué más hacen en San José?

____

6. 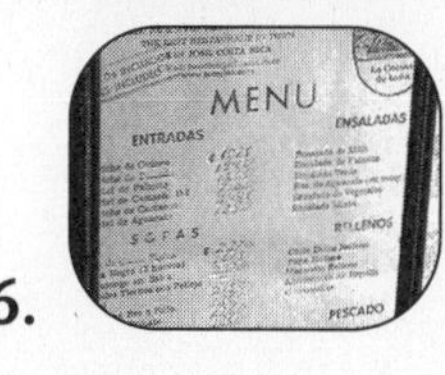

¿Qué es una *soda* en Costa Rica?

____

Realidades A

Capítulo 3B

Nombre ______ Hora ______

Fecha ______

VIDEO

Y, ¿qué más?

Actividad 4

Tomás was confused because he learned that **un refresco** was a soft drink. However, in Costa Rica **un refresco** is fruit juice. Can you think of any examples of English words that have a different meaning depending on where in the United States you go? What are their different meanings?

______

______

______

______

______

______

______

Nombre ______________________ Hora ______________

Fecha ______________________

AUDIO

Actividad 5

Listen to a radio announcer as he interviews people at the mall about their lifestyles. Pay close attention to the things that they say they do and eat. What in their lifestyles is good or bad for their health? Match what they say to the pictures below. Then write the corresponding letter in the appropriate column. You will hear this conversation twice.

ACTIVIDADES

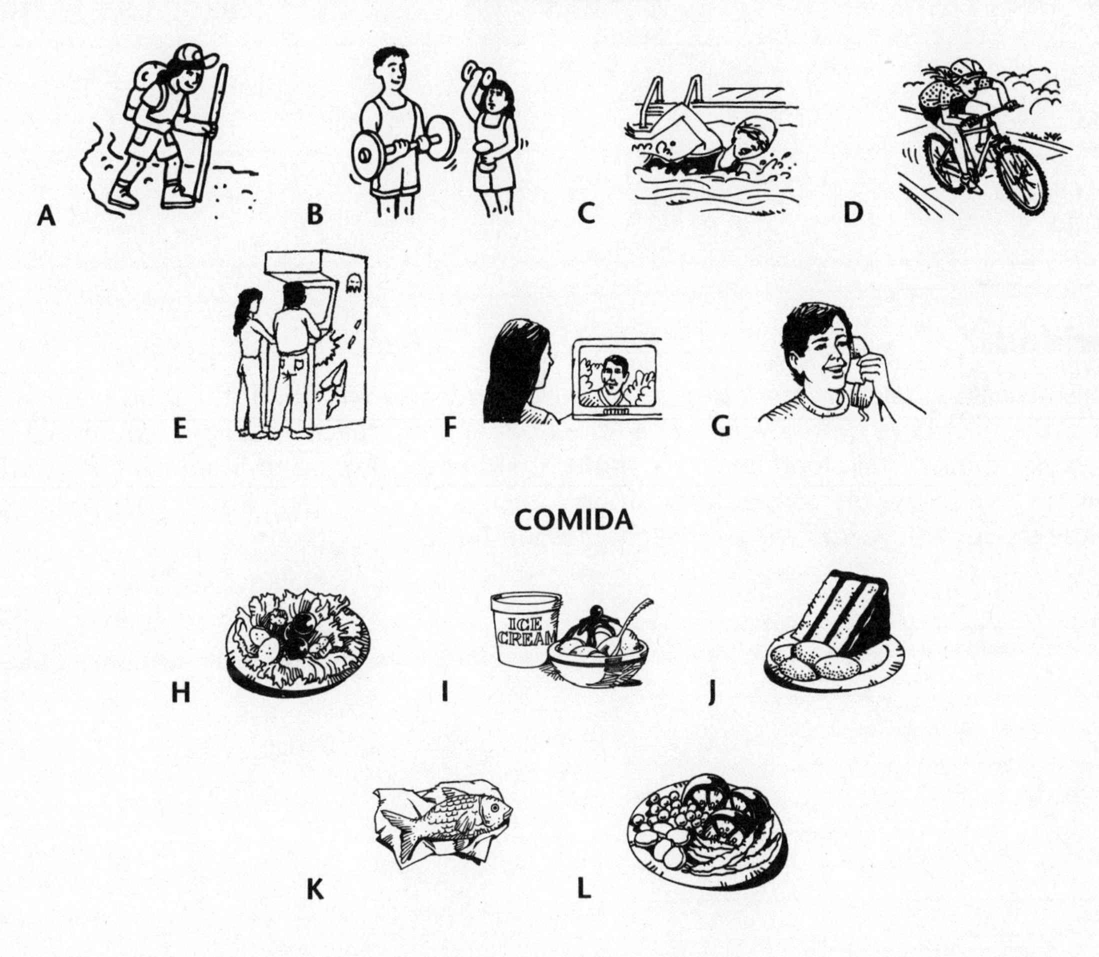

	Bueno para la salud ☺	**Malo para la salud** ☹
1. Mariana	______	______
2. Jorge	______	______
3. Luz	______	______
4. Nacho	______	______

Nombre ______________________ Hora __________

Fecha ______________________

AUDIO

Actividad 6

Listen as students in a health class in Costa Rica present a list of the "dos and don'ts" of staying healthy. Which are **consejos lógicos** (*logical advice*) and which are **consejos ridículos** (*ridiculous advice*)? Place a check mark in the appropriate box of the chart. You will hear each set of statements twice.

	1	2	3	4	5	6	7	8	9	10
Consejo lógico										
Consejo ridículo										

Actividad 7

A Spanish-speaking telemarketer calls your home to interview you about the food preferences of teens. He must have gotten your name from your Spanish teacher! He asks you to tell him whether you think certain food items are **malo** or **sabroso**. Be sure to listen carefully so that you will be able to use the correct form of the adjective for each item. Write what you would say in the spaces below. You will hear each question twice.

1. ______________________
2. ______________________
3. ______________________
4. ______________________
5. ______________________
6. ______________________
7. ______________________
8. ______________________
9. ______________________
10. ______________________

Nombre ______ Hora ______

Fecha ______

AUDIO

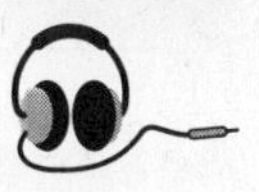

Actividad 8

In an effort to improve food in the school cafeteria, students are asked to anonymously call in their opinions about school food. You are asked to chart the responses of the Spanish-speaking students. As you listen to their opinions, fill in the grid. If they say something positive about a particular menu item, put a plus sign in the appropriate column; if they say something negative, put a minus sign in the column. You will hear each set of statements twice.

1										
2										
3										
4										
5										

Actividad 9

Listen as people call in to ask Dr. Armando their health questions on his radio program **"Pregunte al doctor Armando."** While you listen to their questions and Dr. Armando's advice (**consejo**), fill in the chart below. Do you agree with his advice? You will hear this conversation twice.

NOMBRE	¿LA PREGUNTA?	EL CONSEJO
1. Beatriz		
2. Mauricio		
3. Loli		
4. Luis		

Actividad 10

A. The school nurse has compiled information on what everyone eats and is now telling you which foods are good for your health and which are not. Remember what you wrote for her survey? List the items you eat on a daily basis. Be sure to use words from the previous chapter as well as ones from this chapter.

B. Now, use the information from **MiPlato** and what you know about a well-balanced diet to fill in what the nurse would say. Follow the model.

las verduras

las grasas

las frutas

la carne

Frutas Granos Productos Lácteos Vegetales Proteína

MiPlato
ChooseMyPlate.gov

Modelo *Los espaguetis son buenos para la salud. Ud. debe comer mucho pan y muchos cereales.*

1.

2.

3.

4.

Realidades 

Capítulo 3B

Nombre ______________________ Hora ________

Fecha ______________________

WRITING

Actividad 11

Write your opinions of the following foods. Use the correct forms of the following adjectives in your sentences.

bueno	malo	sabroso	divertido
malo para la salud		bueno para la salud	
interesante		horrible	

Modelo  *Las uvas son sabrosas.*

1. ______________________
2. ______________________
3. ______________________
4. ______________________
5. ______________________
6. ______________________
7. ______________________
8. ______________________

Realidades A — Nombre ______ Hora ______

Capítulo 3B — Fecha ______

WRITING

Actividad 12

Below you see three groups of friends sitting at tables in a cafeteria. Describe the people and items at each table.

Mesa 1:

______

Mesa 2:

______

Mesa 3:

______

Realidades A | Nombre ____ | Hora ____

Capítulo 3B | Fecha ____ | WRITING

Actividad 13

Write a letter to your Spanish-speaking pen pal about a restaurant that you and your parents like to go to for dinner. Tell what you and your family members normally eat and drink, what the food is like, and what the waiters (**camareros**) are like.

Estimado(a) ____________________ :

____

____

____

____

____

____

____

____

____

____

____

____

____

____

____

____

____

____

Un abrazo,

____

Nombre ____________________ Hora __________

Fecha ____________________

VIDEO

Antes de ver el video

Actividad 1

Think of activities you do at different times during the week. Make a list of four activities you do during the week and then four activities you do during the weekend.

Actividades durante la semana	Actividades durante el fin de semana
____________________	____________________
____________________	____________________
____________________	____________________
____________________	____________________

¿Comprendes?

Actividad 2

Javier has just moved to a new high school in Spain, and he is sitting by himself. Ignacio, Elena, and Ana try to find out more about him. What do they do, and what do they learn? Write **cierto** (*true*) or **falso** (*false*) next to each statement.

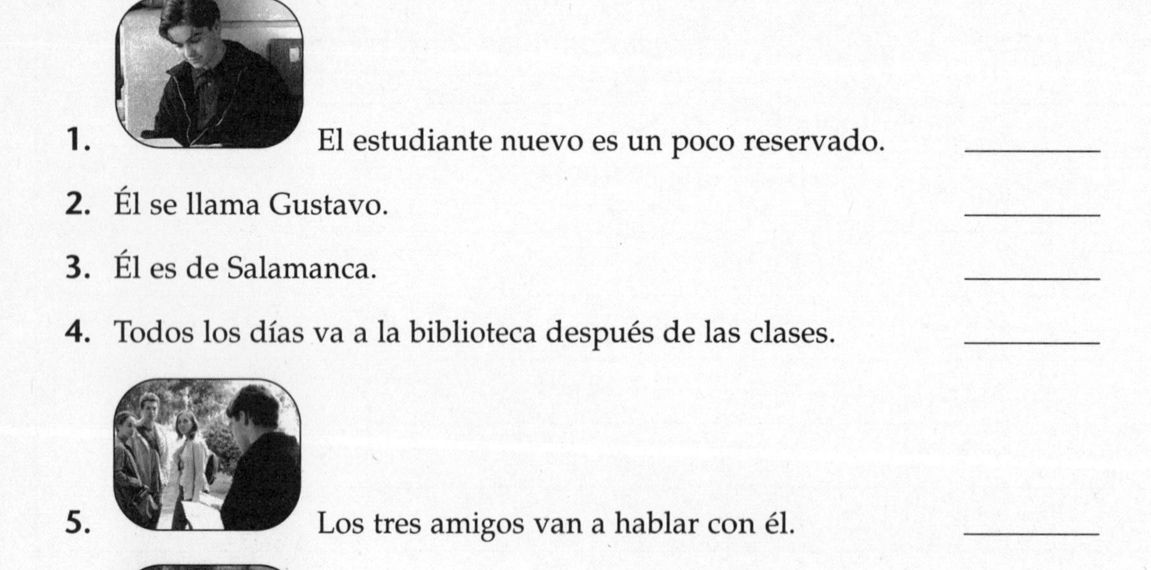

1. El estudiante nuevo es un poco reservado. __________
2. Él se llama Gustavo. __________
3. Él es de Salamanca. __________
4. Todos los días va a la biblioteca después de las clases. __________
5. Los tres amigos van a hablar con él. __________

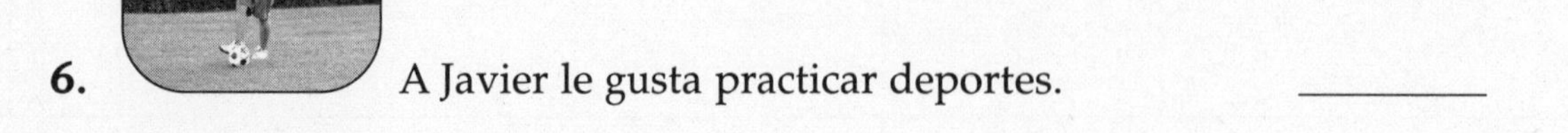

6. A Javier le gusta practicar deportes. __________

7. A veces, él prefiere ir al cine a ver películas. ______

8. A él no le gusta hablar con su amigo Esteban de San Antonio. ______

Actividad 3

What do the new friends do after class? Fill the blanks with complete sentences.

Nuevos amigos	¿Adónde va después de las clases?
1. Javier	
2. Ignacio	
3. Elena	
4. Ana	

Y, ¿qué más?

Actividad 4

What do you do after school every day? What do you sometimes do, and what do you never do at all? Write a short paragraph about your afterschool activities, following the example below.

Modelo *Yo voy a mi trabajo todos los días en el centro comercial. A veces, voy con una amiga al cine después del trabajo. Nunca voy al gimnasio durante la semana.*

Nombre ____________________ Hora ________

Fecha ____________________

AUDIO

Actividad 5

Listen as Lorena talks to Luis and Antonio about where they are going during the week. Under each picture in the grid, write in the name of Luis or Antonio if they tell Lorena they are going to that place. In some cases, you will fill in both of their names. After completing the grid, you will be able to complete the sentences under the grid. You will hear this conversation twice.

	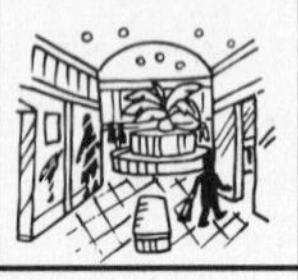	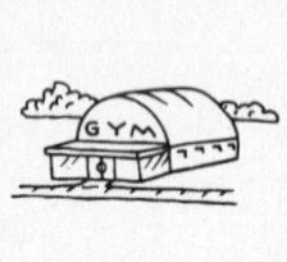	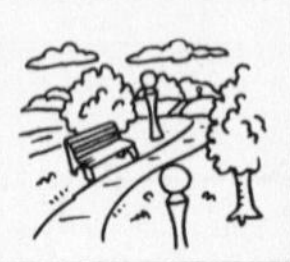	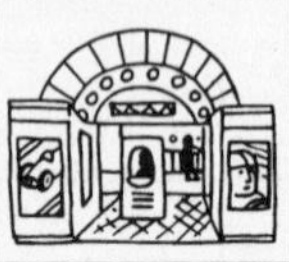	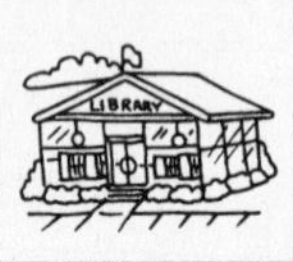	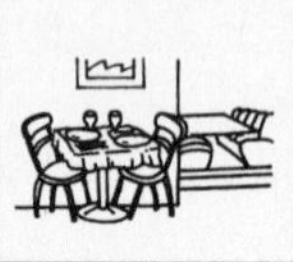	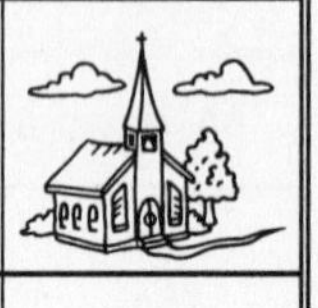
lunes							
martes							
miércoles							
jueves							
viernes							
sábado							
domingo							

1. Luis y Antonio van al (a la) ____________________ el ____________________.
2. También van al (a la) ____________________ el ____________________.

Nombre ____________________ Hora ____________

Fecha ____________________ **AUDIO**

Actividad 6

You are volunteering as a tour guide during the upcoming Hispanic Arts Festival in your community. To make sure you would be able to understand the following questions if a visitor were to ask them, write the number of the question under the correct picture that would correspond to a logical response. You can check your answers to see if you're ready to answer visitors' questions during the Festival. You will hear each question twice.

Actividad 7

Your friend Miguel calls his mother from your house to give her an update on his plans for the day. Just from listening to his side of the conversation, you realize that his mother has LOTS of questions. What does she ask him, based on Miguel's answers? Choose from the following:

A. ¿Adónde vas?

B. ¿Con quiénes vas?

C. ¿Cuándo vas?

D. ¿Cómo es tu amigo?

E. ¿Por qué van?

You will hear each set of statements twice.

1. ________ 2. ________ 3. ________ 4. ________ 5. ________

Nombre ______________________ Hora ________

Fecha ______________________ AUDIO

Actividad 8

The yearbook staff is identifying students' pictures for the yearbook. Look at the pictures from the class trip to Mexico. Listen to the conversations and write the names of Arturo, Susi, Gloria, Martín, David, Eugenia, Enrique, and Lucía under the correct pictures. You will hear each dialogue twice.

Actividad 9

Listen as a radio interviewer talks to Maricela, a young woman from Spain, about her city that was once home to the **Reyes** Fernando and Isabel. You will learn why it is such a popular tourist spot. After listening, answer the questions below. You will hear this conversation twice.

1. Maricela es de
   a) Madrid. b) Aranjuez. c) Barcelona.
2. La ciudad es famosa por
   a) el pescado. b) el helado. c) las fresas.
3. Los turistas van
   a) al palacio. b) a las montañas. c) a la playa.
4. La ciudad de Maricela está a unos ______ minutos de Madrid.
   a) quince b) treinta c) cincuenta
5. Las comidas típicas son
   a) pizza y espaguetis. b) fresas y pasteles de manzana. c) pollo y judías verdes.
6. Maricela va ______ para pasar tiempo con los amigos.
   a) al parque b) al cine c) a las montañas

Nombre ______________________ Hora __________

Fecha ______________________

WRITING

Actividad 10

While on a hike one day, you stumble upon a "Wheel of the Future." When you spin this wheel, you will land on a picture of a place. The wheel will send you to that place if you tell it when you want to go and what you plan to do there. Write what you would tell the wheel for each place. Follow the model.

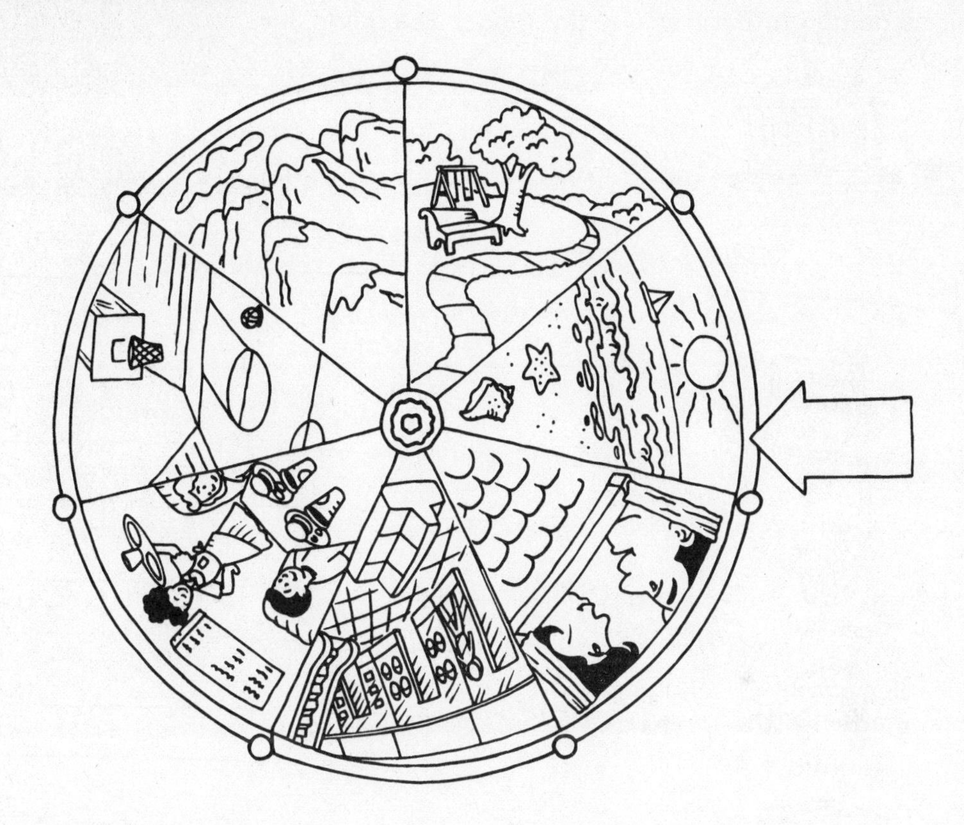

Modelo *Voy a la playa el viernes para nadar.*

1. ______________________________

2. ______________________________

3. ______________________________

4. ______________________________

5. ______________________________

6. ______________________________

7. ______________________________

Actividad 11

You are having a surprise party for your best friend next weekend, and you need to know where your family and friends are going to be this week so that you can get in touch with them to make plans. Below is a planner containing information on everyone's plans for the week. Using the pictures to help you, write where your friends and family will be and what they will be doing on that day. Use the model as a guide.

Modelo YO Lunes: *El lunes yo voy a la biblioteca para hacer la tarea.*

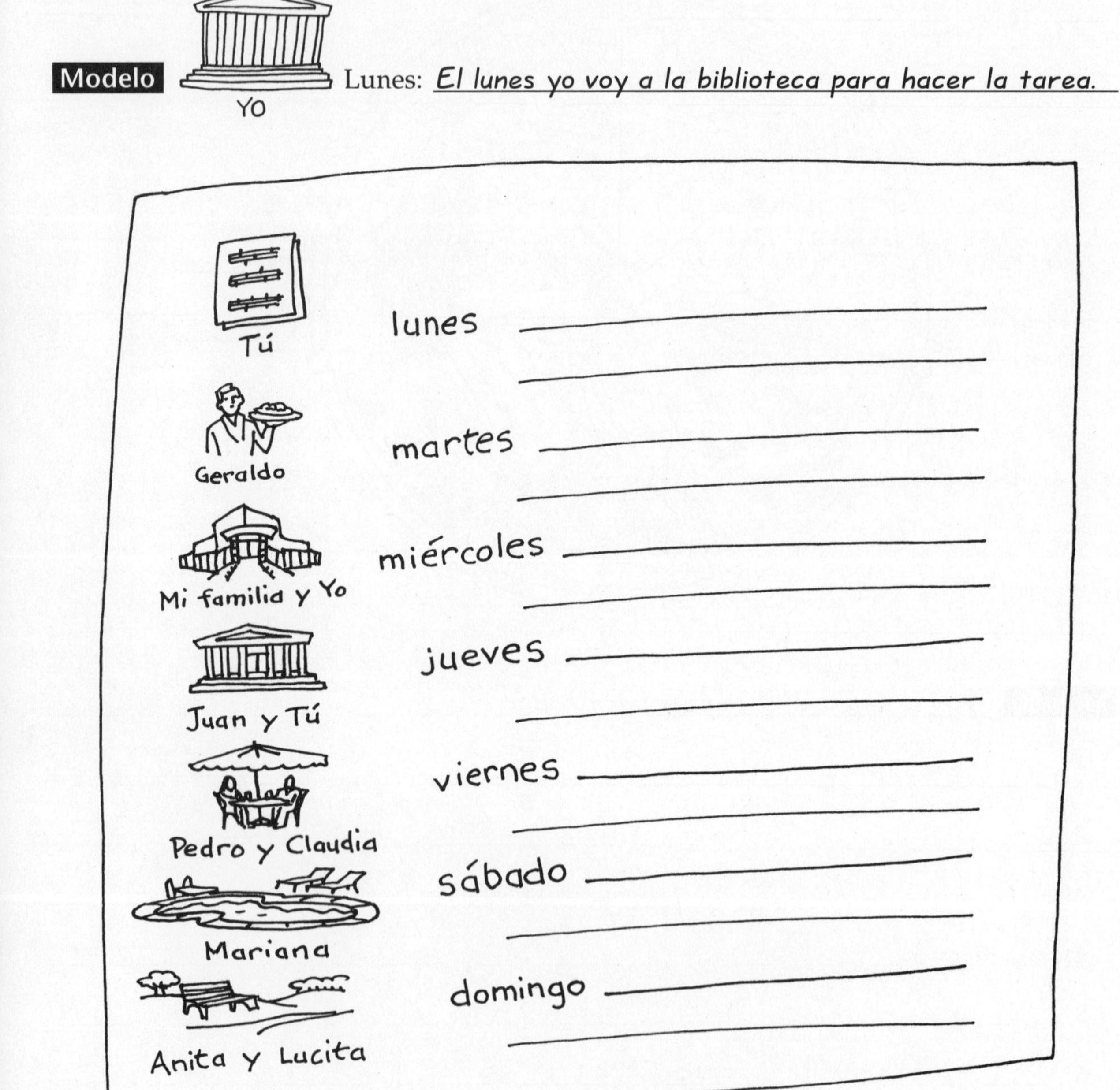

Nombre _______________ Hora _______________

Fecha _______________

WRITING

Actividad 12

You are a contestant on a game show. The host of the show has given you these answers. Write the corresponding questions.

Modelo El catorce de febrero

¿Cuándo es el Día de San Valentín?

1. El primer presidente de los Estados Unidos

____

2. Al norte (*north*) de los Estados Unidos

____

3. Usamos esta cosa para conectar al Internet.

____

4. Muy bien, gracias. ¿Y tú?

____

5. Vamos a la tienda para comprar frutas.

____

6. Las personas que enseñan las clases

____

7. Usamos estas partes del cuerpo para ver.

____

Actividad 13

A. Write four complete sentences that tell about places you and a friend go to on the weekend.

1. ____
2. ____
3. ____
4. ____

Nombre ______ Hora ______

Fecha ______

WRITING

B. Now, use your sentences from Part A to write a paragraph telling with whom you go to these places, what the places are like, and what you do when you are there.

Nombre ______________________ Hora ________

Fecha ______________________

Antes de ver el video

Actividad 1

Think of activities you like to do. Here is a list of six activities. Rank them in order from your favorite to your least favorite, with 1 as your favorite and 6 as your least favorite.

_____ ir a bailar

_____ nadar

_____ estudiar en la biblioteca

_____ ir al cine a ver películas

_____ montar en bicicleta

_____ ir de compras al centro comercial

¿Comprendes?

Actividad 2

Ignacio, Javier, Elena, and Ana are playing soccer at the park. Who makes each statement? Write the name of the person who says each item on the line.

1. "Mañana juego al tenis con mis primos." ______________
2. "Yo también estoy muy cansada y tengo mucha sed." ______________
3. "Prefiero otros deportes, como el fútbol." ______________
4. "¿Sabes jugar también al vóleibol?" ______________
5. "También me gusta ir de pesca." ______________
6.  "Puedes bailar conmigo..." ______________
7. "Lo siento. No sé bailar bien." ______________
8. "Voy a preparar un pastel fabuloso." ______________

Realidades A

Capítulo 4B

Nombre ____________________ Hora ____________

Fecha ____________________

VIDEO

Actividad 3

Look at the activities below, and circle the ones you saw or heard about while watching the video. Then, write the ones that Elena can do well on the lines below.

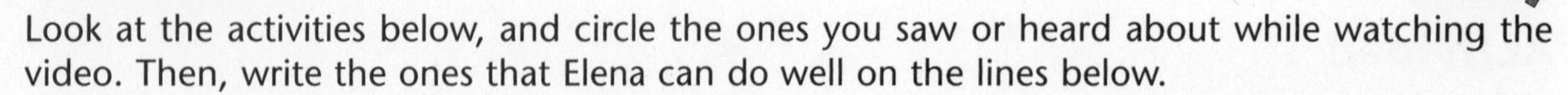

jugar al fútbol	jugar al tenis	ir de cámping	ir de pesca
ir a las fiestas	ver el partido	jugar al vóleibol	
caminar en el parque	jugar al fútbol americano	practicar deportes	
ir al concierto	preparar un pastel	jugar al béisbol	jugar al golf
jugar al básquetbol	bailar y cantar	tomar refrescos	

____

____

Y, ¿qué mas?

Actividad 4

Imagine that Ignacio, Javier, Elena, and Ana want you to join them in their various activities. What answers might you give them? Respond to their invitations with some of the phrases from the video, or make up your own responses from what you have learned. Follow the model.

Modelo ¿Quieres jugar al fútbol en el parque?

Sí, quiero jugar al fútbol en el parque, pero no juego muy bien.

1. ¿Puedes jugar al tenis mañana?

____

2. Oye, juegas muy bien al vóleibol. ¿Puedes jugar más tarde?

____

3. ¿Quieres ir con nosotros a la fiesta esta noche?

____

4. ¿Sabes bailar?

____

Nombre ______________________ Hora ______

Fecha ______________________ AUDIO

Actividad 5

There are not enough hours in the day to do everything we want to do. Listen to the following interviews. What do these people want more time to do? In the blanks provided, write the number of the statement that corresponds to each picture. You will hear each set of statements twice.

Actividad 6

After listening to each of the following statements, decide if you think the excuses given are believable (**creíble**) or unbelievable (**increíble**). Be prepared to defend your answers with a partner after making your decisions. You will hear each set of statements twice.

EXCUSAS, EXCUSAS

	Creíble	Increíble		Creíble	Increíble
1.	❑	❑	5.	❑	❑
2.	❑	❑	6.	❑	❑
3.	❑	❑	7.	❑	❑
4.	❑	❑	8.	❑	❑

Nombre ____________________ Hora __________

Fecha ____________________

AUDIO

Actividad 7

Listen to the following couple as they try to decide what they are going to do tonight. Every time an activity is mentioned that one of the two people is going to do, draw a circle around the picture. If the other person is NOT going to do that activity, draw an *X* through the picture. The pictures with circles only should represent what both people finally decide to do. You will hear each conversation twice.

Actividad 8

Listen as a radio program host interviews a fitness expert, doctora Benítez, about the best way to get in shape. Listen to the **entrevista** (*interview*), and choose the best answer to the questions below. You will hear this conversation twice.

1. ¿En qué es experta la doctora Benítez?
   a) deportes b) cocinar c) música d) ejercicio y nutrición
2. Según la doctora, ¿cuántos minutos de ejercicio debes hacer todos los días?
   a) una hora b) quince minutos c) treinta minutos
3. Según Miguel, ¿por qué no puede hacer mucho ejercicio?
   a) Es demasiado perezoso. b) Está muy ocupado. c) Está triste.
4. ¿Qué es divertido para Miguel?
   a) jugar al tenis b) ver la tele c) jugar al fútbol
5. Después de jugar, ¿qué no debemos comer?
   a) cereales b) frutas y verduras c) pasteles

Nombre _______________ Hora _______________

Fecha _______________ AUDIO

Actividad 9

Your Spanish teacher always encourages you to speak Spanish to your classmates outside of class. In order to do that, you and your friends agreed to talk on the phone and/or leave messages on each other's answering machines for at least a week. Listen to the messages your friends have left on your answering machine today. Based on the messages, decide a) where the person wants to go; b) what the person wants to do; c) what time the person wants to go. Use the chart below to record the information. You will hear each set of statements twice.

	¿Adónde quiere ir?	¿Qué quiere hacer?	¿A qué hora quiere ir?
Justo			
Eva			
José			
Margarita			
Pedro			

Realidades A

Nombre ______________________ Hora ______

Capítulo 4B

Fecha ______________________

WRITING

Actividad 10

A. Read the following announcements of upcoming events in Madrid. Underneath each announcement, write whether or not you are going to each event and why or why not.

UNA NOCHE DE ÓPERA ITALIANA

PRESENTANDO a **JOSÉ CARRERAS** en el Auditorio Nacional de Música, Madrid

el viernes a las siete de la noche

____

____

PARTIDO DE FÚTBOL

REAL BETIS CONTRA REAL MADRID

el domingo a las dos de la tarde en el Estadio Santiago Bernabeu

____

____

Fiesta Deportiva

¿Te gusta practicar deportes? ¿Eres atlético?

Ven a mi fiesta deportiva y puedes jugar varios deportes con muchas personas.

La fiesta es desde el viernes a las cinco de la tarde hasta el lunes a las cinco de la mañana.

____

B. Now, in the spaces below, write whether five people you know are going to any one of the events and why or why not. Follow the model.

Modelo *Mi amiga Ana va al partido de fútbol porque le gusta mucho el fútbol.*

Mi amigo Ronaldo no va al concierto porque no le gusta la ópera.

1. ______________________
2. ______________________
3. ______________________
4. ______________________
5. ______________________

Actividad 11

Every time a classmate asks Eugenio if he wants to do something fun, he declines and gives a different excuse. In the spaces below, write the question that each classmate asks and Eugenio's varying answers. Follow the model.

Modelo

—*¿Vas a levantar pesas conmigo?*

—*No, no puedo levantar pesas porque me duele la cabeza.*

1. —¿ ____________________?
   —No, ____________________.
2. —¿ ____________________?
   —No, ____________________.
3. —¿ ____________________?
   —No, ____________________.
4. —¿ ____________________?
   —No, ____________________.
5. —¿ ____________________?
   —No, ____________________.
6. —¿ ____________________?
   —No, ____________________.
7. —¿ ____________________?
   —No, ____________________.

Realidades A

Capítulo 4B

Nombre ______________________ Hora ______________

Fecha ______________________ **WRITING**

Actividad 12

When put in the right order, each set of blocks below will ask a question. Unscramble the blocks by writing the contents of each block in the blank boxes. Then, answer the questions in the space provided.

1.

J U E G	D E	E P O R	O S F	U É D	A S L
I N E S	¿ A Q	T E S	N A ?	S E M A	

____

____

____

2.

¿ A Q	M I G O	T E S	U S A	J U E G	U É D
S ?	A N T	E P O R			

____

____

____

3.

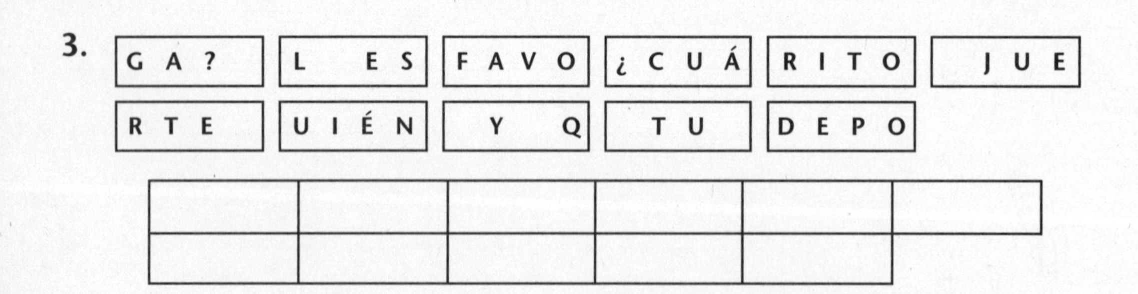

____

____

____

Actividad 13

You are having a mid-semester party.

A. First, fill in the invitation below with the information about your party.

FIESTA DE MEDIO SEMESTRE

Lugar: ______

Hora: ______

Comida: ______

______

RSVP: ______

B. Since you don't have everyone's mailing address, you have to e-mail some people about the party. Write your e-mail below. In addition to inviting them, tell them what activities you will have at the party, and where your house is (**está cerca de la biblioteca,** etc.).

Estimados amigos:

______

¡Me gustaría ver a todos en la fiesta!

Un fuerte abrazo,

______

Notes

Notes

Notes

Notes

Notes

Notes

Notes

Notes

Notes

Notes

Notes

Notes

Notes

Test Preparation

Table of Contents

To the Student

Did you know that becoming a better reader in Spanish can improve your scores on standardized reading tests in English? Research has shown that the skills you develop by reading in a second language are transferred to reading in your first language. Research also shows that the more you practice for standardized tests and work on test-taking strategies, the more your scores will improve. The goal of this book is to help you improve your test-taking strategies and to provide extra practice with readings in both Spanish and English.

Getting to Know the Test

The practice tests in this book offer a variety of readings to reflect the types of passages you might expect to find on a standardized test. They also provide practice for three different types of questions you are apt to encounter on such a test: multiple choice, Short Response, and Extended Response.

Multiple Choice Multiple choice questions always have four answer choices. Pick the one that is the best answer. A correct answer is worth 1 point.

Short Response This symbol appears next to questions requiring short written answers:

This symbol appears next to questions requiring short written answers that are a creative extension based on the reading:

Take approximately 3 to 5 minutes to answer a Short Response question. Read all parts of the question carefully, plan your answer, then write the answer in your own words. A complete answer to a Short Response question is worth 2 points. A partial answer is worth 1 or 0 points.

NOTE: <u>If a Short Response question is written in English, write your answer in English, unless the instructions tell you to do otherwise. If it is written in Spanish, write your answer in Spanish.</u>

Extended Response This symbol appears next to questions requiring longer written answers based on information that can be inferred from the reading:

This symbol appears next to questions requiring longer written answers that are a creative extension based on the reading:

Take approximately 5 to 15 minutes to answer an Extended Response question. A complete answer is worth 4 points. A partial answer is worth 3, 2, 1, or 0 points.

NOTE: <u>If an Extended Response question is written in English, write your answer in English. If it is written in Spanish, write your answer in Spanish.</u>

Taking These Practice Tests

Your teacher will assign a test for classwork or homework, or you might be taking these tests on your own. Each reading is followed by questions, and the Response Sheet immediately follows the questions. For multiple choice questions, you should bubble-in the response. For Short and Extended Response questions, write your answers on the lines provided.

Tips for Improving Your Score

Know the Rules

Learn the rules for any test you take. For example, depending on how a test is scored, it may or may not be advisable to guess if you are not sure of the correct answer. Find that out before you begin the exam. Be sure you understand:

- how much time is allowed for the test
- the types of questions that will be asked
- how the questions should be answered
- how they will be scored

Know Yourself and Make a Plan

Ask yourself: "How will I prepare for the test?" First, ask your teacher to help you list your strengths and weaknesses on tests. Then make a detailed plan for practicing or reviewing. Give yourself plenty of time to prepare. Don't leave everything until the night before. Set aside blocks of uninterrupted time for studying, with short breaks at regular intervals.

Before the Test

Do something relaxing the night before. Then get a good night's sleep, and be sure to eat a nutritious meal before the test. Wear comfortable clothing. If possible, wear a watch or sit where you can see a clock. Make sure you have all the materials you will need. Find out in advance if you will need a certain type of pencil, for example, and bring several with you—already sharpened. Be sure you know where the test is being given and at what time. Plan to arrive early.

Know What You Are Being Asked

There are two basic types of test questions: objective, one-right-answer questions and essay questions. It is essential that you read all questions carefully. Ask yourself, "What are they asking me?" The purpose of a standardized reading test is to determine:

- how well you understand what you read
- how well you are able to use the critical thinking and problem-solving skills that are so critical for success in today's world

Here is a list of basic reading skills:

- Understanding major ideas, details, and organization
- Drawing conclusions
- Understanding cause and effect
- Comparing and contrasting
- Finding, interpreting, and organizing information
- Understanding author's purpose and/or viewpoint
- Understanding character and plot development

Always read the questions before you read the passage. This will help you focus on the task. If it is allowed, ask your teacher to explain any directions you do not understand.

Watch Your Time

Allot a specific amount of time per question—approximately 1 minute for multiple choice, 3 to 5 minutes for Short Response, and 5 to 15 minutes for Extended Response. Do not spend too much time on any one question, and monitor your time so that you will be able to complete the test.

Show What You Know, Relax, and Think Positively

Answer those questions that you are sure about first. If a question seems too difficult, skip it and return to it later. Remember that while some questions may seem hard, others will be easy. You may never learn to love taking tests, but you can control the situation and make sure that you reach your full potential for success.

Above all, relax. It's natural to be nervous, but think positively. Just do your best.

Multiple Choice Questions: Helpful Hints

Multiple choice questions have only one right answer. There is no "creative" response, only a correct one. This book provides extensive practice for the types of multiple choice items that you might find on a standardized reading test. There are four answer choices (A, B, C, D or F, G, H, J) per question. Allot approximately 1 minute to answer a multiple choice question. Answers are worth 1 point each.

- Read the question carefully.
- Try to identify the answer <u>before</u> you examine the choices.
- Eliminate obviously incorrect choices by lightly crossing them out.
- Try to narrow the choices down to two.
- Depending on how a test is to be scored, you may or may not want to guess (for these practice tests, check that you will **not** be penalized for guessing wrong).

Short and Extended Response: Helpful Hints

The dreaded essay question will probably not be as difficult as expected if you follow these strategies:

- Read the question <u>before</u> reading the passage.
- Re-read the question as you prepare to respond: Are you being asked to list, describe, explain, discuss, persuade, or compare and contrast? These are very different things.
- Look back at the passage as often as necessary to answer the question correctly. Underline any key sections that you think might be important to your response.
- Use the margins next to the passage to jot down thoughts and ideas and to prepare a brief outline of what you will include in your answer. Use a clear, direct introduction that answers the specific question being asked. As a start, try turning the question into a statement. Include both general ideas and specific details from the reading in your answer.

- Review your response to make sure you have expressed your thoughts well. Is your introduction clear? Have you stated the general idea(s)? Have you included supporting details?
- If your response is in Spanish, check for grammar errors (subject-verb agreement, adjective agreement, correct verb endings and tenses). In either language, proofread your answer for correct spelling.

How the Test Will Be Scored

It is important to know in advance how responses will be scored. This will lower your anxiety level and help you focus. For the purpose of these practice tests, you can assume the following:

Multiple Choice Questions

Multiple choice answers are either right or wrong. You will receive credit and 1 point if you select the correct answer.

Performance-Based Questions (Short and Extended Response)

Short and Extended Response questions are called "performance tasks." They are often scored with rubrics, which describe a range of performance. You will receive credit for how close your answers come to the desired response. The performance tasks on these practice tests will require thoughtful answers. You must:

- Read the passage
- Think about the question as it relates to the passage, and
- Explain your answer by citing general ideas and specific details from the passage

or:

- Create a written document (a letter, for example) that clearly uses or models information provided in the reading passage

Rubric for Short Response Questions

2 points The response indicates that the student has a complete understanding of the reading concept embodied in the task. The student has provided a response that is accurate, complete, and fulfills all the requirements of the task. Necessary support and/or examples are included, and the information given is clearly text-based. Any extensions beyond the text are relevant to the task.

1 point The response indicates that the student has a partial understanding of the reading concept embodied in the task. The student has provided a response that may include information that is essentially correct and text-based, but the information is too general or too simplistic. Some of the support and/or examples may be incomplete or omitted.

0 points The response is inaccurate, confused, and/or irrelevant, or the student has failed to respond to the task.

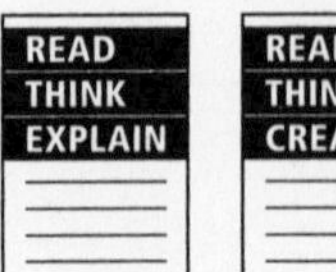

Rubric for Extended Response Questions

4 points The response indicates that the student has a thorough understanding of the reading concept embodied in the task. The student has provided a response that is accurate, complete, and fulfills all the requirements of the task. Necessary support and/or examples are included, and the information given is clearly text-based. Any extensions beyond the text are relevant to the task.

3 points The response indicates that the student has an understanding of the reading concept embodied in the task. The student has provided a response that is accurate and fulfills all the requirements of the task, but the required support and/or details are not complete or clearly text-based.

2 points The response indicates that the student has a partial understanding of the reading concept embodied in the task. The student has provided a response that may include information that is essentially correct and text-based, but the information is too general or too simplistic. Some of the support and/or examples and requirements of the task may be incomplete or omitted.

1 point The response indicates that the student has very limited understanding of the reading concept embodied in the task. The response is incomplete, may exhibit many flaws, and may not address all requirements of the task.

0 points The response is inaccurate, confused, and/or irrelevant, or the student has failed to respond to the task.

Getting Started

So let's get started. If there was anything in this Introduction that you did not understand, ask your teacher about it. Glance once again at the Helpful Hints before taking the first test. In fact, it will be helpful if you review those hints each time you take one of these tests. And remember: The more you practice, the higher your scores will be.

¡Buena suerte!

Realidades A

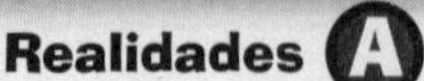

Integrated Performance Assessment

Unit theme: En la escuela, En la clase, El tiempo

Context for the Integrated Performance Assessment: Your Spanish teacher wants you to know why Spanish is an important and useful language to learn.

Interpretive Task: Watch the video "Why Study Spanish?" found on *Realidades 1, DVD 1, Capítulo 1A.* Make a list of professions where knowing Spanish has been an asset.

Interpersonal Task: Discuss the professions you learned about on the video with two other students. Brainstorm other careers or situations in which Spanish could also be an asset.

Presentational Task: Present your ideas to the class as a whole. Have a fellow student or the teacher note all the possible uses on the board so that the students can copy the complete list and keep it in their notebooks for future reference.

Interpersonal Task Rubric

	Score: 1 Does not meet expectations	Score: 3 Meets expectations	Score: 5 Exceeds expectations
Content Comprehension	Student includes few of the professions mentioned in the video and brainstorms no additional careers and situations.	Student includes some of the professions mentioned in the video and brainstorms some additional careers and situations.	Student includes all of the professions mentioned in the video and brainstorms many additional careers and situations.
Group Participation	Student participates poorly with the group.	Student participates well with the group.	Student participates very well with the group.

Presentational Task Rubric

	Score: 1 Does not meet expectations	Score: 3 Meets expectations	Score: 5 Exceeds expectations
Amount of Communication	Student gives limited or no details or examples.	Student gives adequate details or examples.	Student gives consistent details or examples.
Comprehensibility	Student's ideas lack clarity and are difficult to understand.	Student's ideas are adequately clear and fairly well understood.	Student's ideas are precise and easily understood.

Realidades A | Nombre ______ | Fecha ______

Capítulo 1A **Reading Skills: Conexiones, p. 41**

Determining the Main Idea

To determine the main idea of the reading passage, the reader must be able to describe what a reading passage is about and summarize it in one sentence. A common problem for students when working with this skill is confusing an important detail in the reading passage with the main idea. Just because something is mentioned in the reading passage does not mean it is the main idea of the passage. Many times the main idea is not even stated in the reading passage. This is called an implied main idea. Regardless of whether the main idea is stated or implied, the basic question remains the same: "What is this reading passage about?"

Tip

Readers are more likely to understand a reading passage when it deals with a topic with which you are already familiar. This familiarity with a topic is known as the reader's prior knowledge. Activating your prior knowledge before reading is one way to improve your understanding of a reading passage. One popular method of activating your prior knowledge is completing a K-W-L chart.

1. Before reading the **Conexiones,** ***"El baile y la música del mundo hispano"*** on page 41 in your textbook, complete the K and W portions of the chart. After you have written down your responses, share them with a classmate. Then read ***"El baile y la música del mundo hispano."*** on page 41 in your textbook. After reading, complete the L portion of the chart.

K **What I Already Know**	**W** **What I Want to Know**	**L** **What I Learned from Reading**
List 3 things you already know about the topic "El baile y la música del mundo hispano."	*List 3 things that you would like to know about the topic* "El baile y la música del mundo hispano."	*List 2 important details that you learned from your reading. Then state in 1 sentence what the reading passage* "El baile y la música del mundo hispano" *is about.*
1. ______	1. ______	1. ______
2. ______	2. ______	2. ______
3. ______	3. ______	3. This passage was mostly about ______

Sample question:

2. What is the main idea of the passage *"El baile y la música del mundo hispano"*?
   A Salsa is the most popular dance in Puerto Rico.
   B Percussion is very important in the music and dance of the Spanish-speaking world.
   C The countries of the Spanish-speaking world have distinct musical styles and traditions.
   D The dances and rhythms of the Spanish-speaking world are not well known in the USA.

Strategies to Analyze Words: Context and Word Structure Clues

It is impossible to know the meaning of every word in a language. However, good readers develop strategies to determine the meanings of unknown words that they encounter in their reading without having to look them up in their dictionaries. Good readers also know that their guesses can be wrong. They then use more traditional methods of finding the word's meaning: looking it up in the dictionary or asking assistance from someone trustworthy.

Both Spanish and English inherited many words from Latin. If you have knowledge of Latin root words, prefixes, and suffixes, you can often make educated guesses about the meaning of words that contain them. Let's take a look at the Latin root words *manus* and *ped* and how they still have meaning for speakers of English and Spanish.

Latin root	English meaning	Spanish meaning	Related words in English and Spanish
manus	hand	*mano*	manual labor/*trabajo manual* = work done by hand
ped	foot	*pie*	pedestrian/*peatón* = someone who travels on foot

Words such as "manual" that look alike and have similar meanings are called cognates.

Tip

Just because a word in Spanish looks like a word in English, the two words are not always cognates. One famous mistake for beginning Spanish students is to try to communicate: "I am embarrassed" by saying, *"Yo estoy embarazada"* which means "I am pregnant" in Spanish! Similarly, an English speaker who assumes that every word in English that contains *ped* has to relate to feet would be mistaken. A pediatrician is not a foot doctor, but a doctor for children.

When making an educated guess about an unusual word, good readers will always test their guess in context. In other words, you will insert your guessed meaning into the actual sentence where you found the unusual word.

1. On page 47 of your textbook, re-read the note written by Pablo from Guinea Ecuatorial. He says, *"No me gusta ni jugar videojuegos ni ver la tele."* If you know that the word *ver* means "to see" or "to watch" in English, what is the most likely meaning of *la tele*?
a. the telephone **b.** the telegraph **c.** the television **d.** the teller

Sample question:

2. The Latin prefix *bi-* relates to the number "two" in English. In which of the following sentences does the word containing the letters *b-i-* actually have a meaning relating to the number "two"? (Remember to use context clues.)
A I was tired of living in a small apartment so I decided to move into something bigger.
B The bison was one of the largest mammals to live on the North American continent.
C Now that I can speak Spanish and English, I am bilingual.
D Biology was my favorite subject in school.

Integrated Performance Assessment
Unit theme: ¿Qué te gusta hacer?

Context for the Integrated Performance Assessment: Since it is early in the school year, you want to learn a little about your classmates.

Interpretive Task: Watch the *Videohistoria: ¿Qué te gusta hacer?* from *Realidades 1, DVD 1, Capítulo 1A.* As you watch, write down 2 activities from the video that you like to do.

Interpersonal Task: Work with a partner and tell him/her the 2 activities you like to do. Ask your partner if he/she likes to do other activities until each of you has 5 different activities on your list.

Presentational Task: Introduce yourself to your classmates and tell them 5 activities you like to do.

Interpersonal Task Rubric

	Score: 1 Does not meet expectations	**Score: 3 Meets expectations**	**Score: 5 Exceeds expectations**
Language Use	Student uses little or no target language and relies heavily on native language word order.	Student uses the target language consistently, but may mix native and target language word order.	Student uses the target language exclusively and integrates target language word order into conversation.
Vocabulary Use	Student uses limited and repetitive language.	Student uses only recently acquired vocabulary.	Student uses both recently and previously acquired vocabulary.

Presentational Task Rubric

	Score: 1 Does not meet expectations	**Score: 3 Meets expectations**	**Score: 5 Exceeds expectations**
Amount of Communication	Student names fewer than five activities that he/she likes to do.	Student names five activities that he/she likes to do.	Student names more than than five activities that he/she likes to do.
Accuracy	Student's accuracy with vocabulary and structures is limited.	Student's accuracy with vocabulary and structures is adequate.	Student's accuracy with vocabulary and structures is exemplary.
Comprehensibility	Student's ideas lack clarity and are difficult to understand.	Student's ideas are adequately clear and fairly well understood.	Student's ideas are precise and easily understood.
Vocabulary Use	Student uses limited and repetitive vocabulary.	Student uses only recently acquired vocabulary.	Student uses both recently and previously acquired vocabulary.

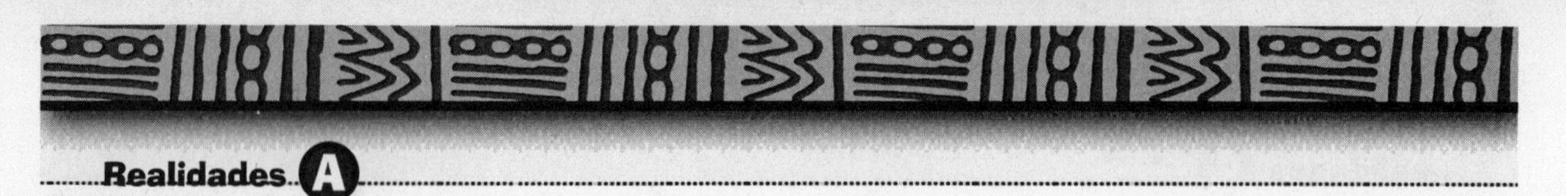

Friendship Among Latin Americans

1 Adriana and Ricardo are teenagers who immigrated to Florida from the Dominican Republic and Mexico. Adriana comes from Santo Domingo, the capital of the Dominican Republic, and Ricardo from Saltillo, Mexico. They have become friends in part because they share a sense of humor and a great love of soccer, a sport they both played in their home countries.

2 For most young Latin Americans, two very strong influences in their lives are family and a close-knit group of friends. Adriana and Ricardo have friends from a number of Spanish-speaking countries, including Guatemala, Colombia, and El Salvador. In the group are several sets of brothers and sisters, and, as is common in Latin America, they all do things together. For example, Adriana (age 14) and her sister Elena (age 12) are very close and share their social lives as well as their family life.

3 Close friendships are sometimes marked by *apodos*, or nicknames, that imply a special relationship. In Mexico, for example, *primo* and *prima* ("cousin") or *hermano* and *hermana* ("brother," "sister") are commonly used. At school, Ricardo often greets Adriana in the halls with "*¡Oye, prima!*"

4 These friends spend free time at each other's homes and they all know each other's families. Close friends are often included in family events and celebrations. Parties that Adriana, Ricardo, and their friends attend may include several generations, from babies to grandparents.

5 Young people, however, must show respect to adults and are taught to treat their parents' friends courteously. They must address them with *usted*. In certain regions of some countries, such as Mexico, Nicaragua, and Colombia, small children may even address their parents with *usted*. In these cases, a young child is also addressed with *usted* as he or she is learning to speak. The difference between *usted* and *tú* is learned later, as the children interact with playmates.

6 In Latin America, many children attend private schools from kindergarten through high school. Because of this, and because a family most likely will not move but will remain in the same home for many years, children who begin kindergarten together often remain classmates throughout their school years. As a result, lifelong friendships can begin at an early age.

Practice Test

Answer questions 1–5. Base your answers on the reading *"Friendship Among Latin Americans."*

1 Where are Adriana and Ricardo currently living?

- **A** the United States
- **B** the Dominican Republic
- **C** Mexico
- **D** Adriana in Santo Domingo and Ricardo in Saltillo

2 In the reading, which of these words is a synonym for ¡Oye! in paragraph 3?

- **F** *Buenos días*
- **G** *Buenas noches*
- **H** *Hola*
- **J** *Mucho gusto*

3 Based on the reading, which one of the following statements is true?

- **A** When they come to the United States, Spanish speakers are friendly mostly with people who came from the same country they did.
- **B** To a Latin American, a friend is almost like a member of the family.
- **C** Latin Americans do not address each other as *tú* until they are adults.
- **D** There are no public schools in Latin America.

4 According to the reading, which of the following is a reason why lifelong friendships can be very common in Latin America?

- **F** Most of your friends would be family members.
- **G** Most Latin Americans have a sense of humor and share an interest in soccer.
- **H** You would probably go to school together from kindergarten through high school.
- **J** You would always treat each other courteously.

5 

From an early age, Latin Americans tend to socialize with people older and younger than they are, as well as with people their own age. Describe what you think might be some advantages of this. If you think there are disadvantages, describe those as well. Use details and information from the reading to support your answer.

Realidades 

Nombre ______________________ Fecha ______________

Capítulo 1A — Practice Test Answer Sheet

1 Ⓐ Ⓑ Ⓒ Ⓓ   2 Ⓕ Ⓖ Ⓗ Ⓙ   3 Ⓐ Ⓑ Ⓒ Ⓓ

4 Ⓕ Ⓖ Ⓗ Ⓙ

5

READ
THINK
EXPLAIN

Drawing Conclusions

To draw a conclusion is to form an opinion based on evidence. If you watch television crime shows, then you have seen detectives analyze a crime scene to form an opinion or draw a conclusion. Readers are often asked to draw conclusions about what they have read. This task often asks readers to determine if there is enough evidence present in the text to support a certain conclusion.

Conclusion statements are rarely right or wrong; they are often presented as believable or not. If you are successful at drawing conclusions from your reading, then you likely are skilled at finding evidence in your reading that supports your conclusions. In addition, conclusions are only as strong as the evidence upon which they are based. Readers must also be willing to change their conclusions as more evidence becomes available in the text.

Tip

One strategy that helps you draw conclusions is a two-column note activity known as Opinion-Proof. As students read, they formulate opinions about what they have read. They write these down on the Opinion side of their notes. If their opinions are believable, then they should be able to write down on the Proof side all the evidence they find in the reading passage that lends support to their opinion.

1. On page 69 of your textbook, re-read the *diamante* poem *"Soy Elena"*. Based on what you have read, fill in the Opinion-Proof chart below.

Opinion	Proof
Elena probably doesn't like talking out loud in class.	______
Elena ______ ______.	*No soy ni deportista ni artística.*
Don't be surprised if Elena takes you up on a dare.	______

Sample question:

2. Read the *diamante* poem "I am James" and answer the question that follows.

I am James,
no job, but busy.
On the beach, if it's sunny.
No worry, I have money.
They say I'm funny.
I'm James.

Based on the evidence presented in the poem "I am James", which conclusion below is the most believable?

A James earns most of his money from selling beach equipment.
B James is bored with his life.
C If it is raining, James will not be at the beach.
D In school, James was known as the class clown.

Reading Skills: Fondo cultural, p. 77

Determining the Author's Point of View

To determine the author's point of view in a reading selection, the reader must figure out how the author feels about a subject in this selection. Readers should first be able to identify when an author feels positive, negative, or neutral toward a subject. As readers gain more practice with this skill, they should then be able to identify a wide range of emotions or attitudes shown by authors. Some of these might include: admiration, nostalgia, sarcasm, surprise, and sympathy.

Tip

To figure out the author's point of view toward his or her subject, try to locate words, phrases, or sentences in the text that have positive or negative associations or connotations. For example, consider the sets of words listed below in Columns A, B, and C. Which one of the words sounds more positive? Which sounds more negative? Which sounds more neutral?

Column A	Column B	Column C
1. denim pants	**1.** faded jeans	**1.** hand-me-downs
2. cafeteria food	**2.** lunch time	**2.** five-star meal
3. classic car	**3.** used car	**3.** mid-size car

1. On page 77 of your textbook, reread the **Fondo cultural** about *huipiles*. Look at the words below from the passage and place a **+** sign next to any word that has positive connotations, a – sign next to any word with negative connotations, and a **0** next to any word where the connotations seem to be neutral.

______ colorful

______ hand-woven

______ weaving

______ unique

Sample question:

2. In the **Fondo cultural**, which word best describes the author's point of view about the *huipiles* worn by the female descendants of the Maya?

A amazed
B sarcastic
C indifferent
D appreciative

Realidades A

Capítulo 1B

Integrated Performance Assessment

Unit theme: Y tú, ¿cómo eres?

Context for the Integrated Performance Assessment: You are going on an exchange program in Mexico for a week. Your host family is looking forward to meeting you and would like to know a little about you.

Interpretive Task: Watch the *Videohistoria: Amigos por Internet* from *Realidades 1, DVD 1, Capítulo 1B.* Notice how the students introduce and describe themselves. Write a brief introduction and description of yourself.

Interpersonal Task: Read your introduction and description to a friend in Spanish class. Ask each other about activities that you do and do not like to do.

Presentational Task: Write an e-mail to your host sister or brother introducing and describing yourself. Include at least 2 activities that you like to do and 2 that you do not like to do.

Interpersonal Task Rubric

	Score: 1 Does not meet expectations	Score: 3 Meets expectations	Score: 5 Exceeds expectations
Language Use	Student uses little or no target language and relies heavily on native language word order.	Student uses the target language consistently, but may mix native and target language word order.	Student uses the target language exclusively and integrates target language word order into conversation.
Vocabulary Use	Student uses limited and repetitive language.	Student uses only recently acquired vocabulary.	Student uses both recently and previously acquired vocabulary.

Presentational Task Rubric

	Score: 1 Does not meet expectations	Score: 3 Meets expectations	Score: 5 Exceeds expectations
Amount of Communication	Student gives limited or no details or examples.	Student gives adequate details or examples.	Student gives consistent details or examples.
Accuracy	Student's accuracy with vocabulary and structures is limited.	Student's accuracy with vocabulary and structures is adequate.	Student's accuracy with vocabulary and structures is exemplary.
Comprehensibility	Student's ideas lack clarity and are difficult to understand.	Student's ideas are adequately clear and fairly well understood.	Student's ideas are precise and easily understood.
Vocabulary Use	Student uses limited and repetitive vocabulary.	Student uses only recently acquired vocabulary.	Student uses both recently and previously acquired vocabulary.

¡Hola! Me llamo Pedro

30 de septiembre

Srta. María Luisa Pardo Barros
Calle San Antonio 16
Valparaíso
Chile

Querida María Luisa:

Me llamo Peter (Pedro en español) y soy de los Estados Unidos. Soy estudiante en Orlando, en el estado de la Florida. Hay muchas atracciones en Orlando: Por ejemplo, el famoso parque de diversiones Disney World —y Sea World también.

Soy muy deportista y me encanta nadar y patinar. Mi mamá dice que soy desordenado y que no soy nada serio. Pero sí me gusta ir a la escuela y me gusta mucho leer buenos libros. ¿Mi actividad favorita? Estar con mis amigos o hablar con ellos por teléfono.

¿Cómo eres, María Luisa?

Tu amigo,

Peter (o Pedro, si el nombre español te gusta más)

Practice Test

Answer questions 1–5. Base your answers on the reading *"¡Hola! Me llamo Pedro."*

1 In what city does María Luisa live?

- **A** San Antonio
- **B** Valparaíso
- **C** Orlando
- **D** The reading does not say.

2 What is the English equivalent of *Querida?*

- **F** Miss
- **G** Hello
- **H** Dear
- **J** It is María Luisa's first name and has no real English equivalent.

3 According to the reading, which one of the following statements might Peter make about himself?

- **A** *Me gusta cocinar.*
- **B** *Me gusta mucho practicar deportes.*
- **C** *No me gusta nada estudiar.*
- **D** *No soy ni serio ni trabajador.*

4 According to the reading, which one of the following words would Peter use to describe himself?

- **F** *reservado*
- **G** *perezoso*
- **H** *sociable*
- **J** *atrevido*

5 READ THINK CREATE

Write a brief letter in Spanish to a pen pal describing yourself and what you like and don't like to do. Use the reading as a model for your letter.

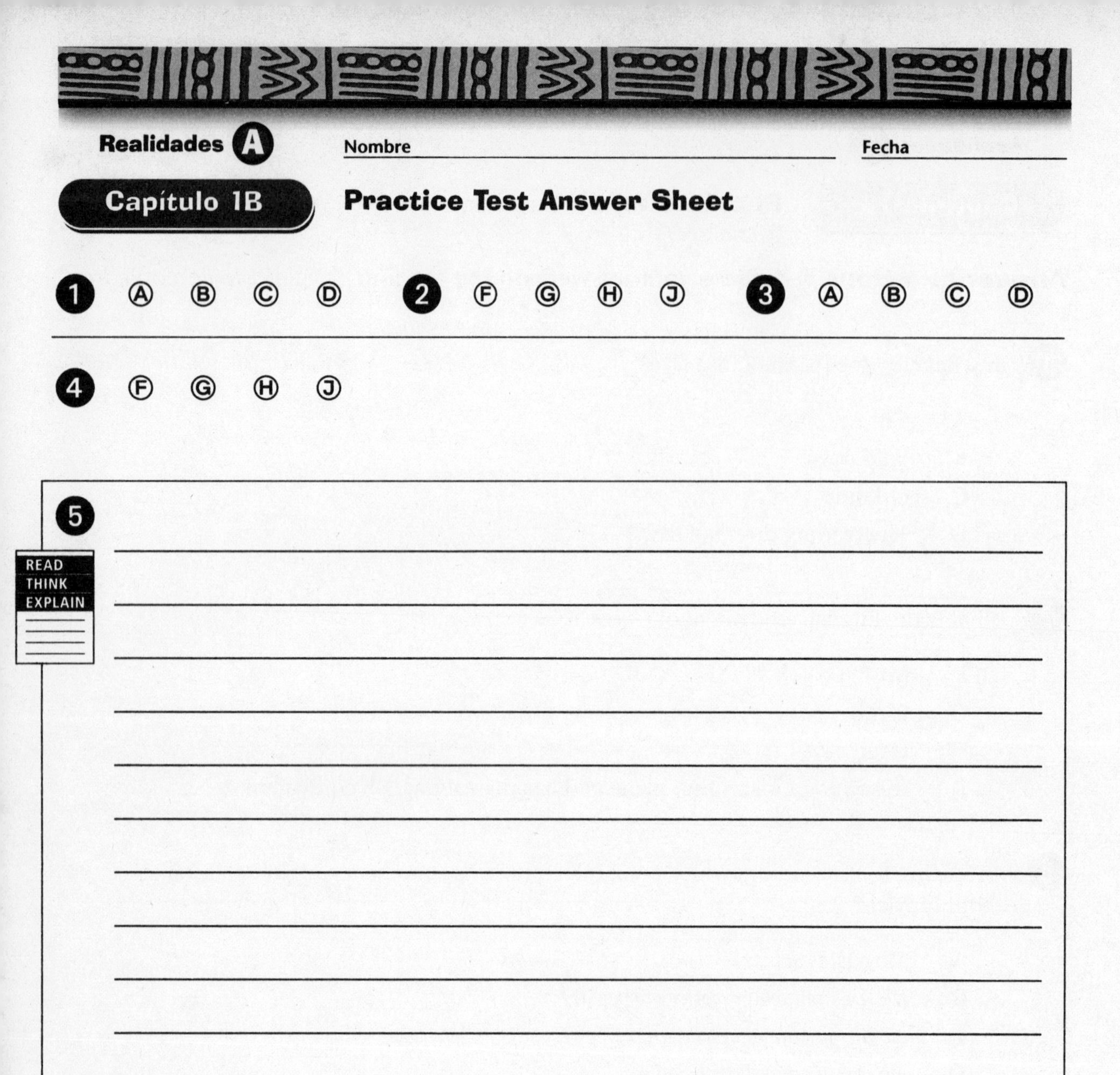

Realidades A

Nombre ______________________ Fecha ______________

Capítulo 1B

Practice Test Answer Sheet

1 Ⓐ Ⓑ Ⓒ Ⓓ 2 Ⓕ Ⓖ Ⓗ Ⓙ 3 Ⓐ Ⓑ Ⓒ Ⓓ

4 Ⓕ Ⓖ Ⓗ Ⓙ

5

READ THINK EXPLAIN

Realidades **A** Nombre ________________ Fecha ________

Capítulo 2A

Reading Skills: Exploración del lenguaje, p. 94
Fondo cultural, p. 95

Recognizing Cause-Effect Relationships

To recognize cause-effect relationships in fiction, nonfiction, drama, or poetry, readers should be aware of why things happen (causes) as well as the consequences or results of actions (effects) in a reading passage.

Tip

To become familiar with this skill, readers should be able to identify certain words or phrases that are often used to show cause-effect relationships. You should also be able to use these words or phrases to describe what you have read in a reading passage.

Here are some common cause-effect words or phrases grouped by similarity in meaning:

because	hence	since
due to	therefore	so that
as a result	thus	consequently

1. On pages 94–95 of your textbook, re-read the two sections, **Exploración del lenguaje** and the **Fondo cultural.** After you have finished reading, complete the sentences below.

   Because Spain was once part of the Roman Empire, ____________________
   ____.

   ____
   ____________________________________; **consequently,**
   September and *septiembre* actually mean "the seventh month."

   ____
   ____________________________________. **As a result,**
   one can find a Roman aqueduct towering over the modern Spanish city of Segovia.

Sample question:

2. Why do December and *diciembre* contain the Latin root word meaning "ten"?
   A Because Spain was once part of the Roman Empire.
   B Because in the Roman calendar there were only ten days in December.
   C Because in the Roman calendar, December was actually the tenth month.
   D Because the number ten was used to indicate the coldest month.

Reading Skills: Lectura, pp. 108–109

Analyzing the Validity and Reliability of Information

When good readers analyze information for validity and reliability, one of the most important questions that they ask themselves is: "How do I know that I can trust that this information is true or accurate?" After answering this question, readers need to determine how such information can be used.

Tip

One way to check a reading passage for validity and reliability is to distinguish between the statements in the passage that are facts and those that are opinions. Readers generally trust factual information more than they trust opinions. A factual statement generally can be put to a test to prove whether the statement is true or false. Statements that involve numbers and/or measurements are more likely to be facts than opinions. Opinions are generally statements that could be interpreted differently by different people.

Let's look at two examples concerning the weather:

A It is 80 degrees Fahrenheit today in San José, Costa Rica.
B It is very hot out today in San José.

With a thermometer, one could easily prove if the temperature in San José is 80 degrees Fahrenheit today. However, the word "hot" in statement B could be interpreted differently by different people. For example, some people might say that 80 degrees is too hot while others might say that 80 degrees is warm. Hence, statement A sounds more factual while statement B sounds more like an opinion.

1. On pages 108–109 of your textbook, re-read the **Lectura, *La Escuela Español Vivo.*** After you have finished reading, read the statements below and identify them as facts or as opinions.

   ________________ Hay clases de música y baile.
   ________________ Los sábados y los domingos hay actividades muy interesantes.
   ________________ El horario del almuerzo es de 13:00 a 14:00.
   ________________ Es una experiencia fabulosa en Costa Rica.

Sample question:

2. Imagine you are interested in improving your Spanish-speaking ability by studying at the **Escuela Español Vivo** in Santa Ana, Costa Rica. Which statement from the brochure would be of most interest to you?
   A Visitar un volcán.
   B Mucha práctica y conversación en español.
   C Una experiencia fabulosa en Costa Rica.
   D Amigos de muchos países.

Realidades A

Capítulo 2A

Integrated Performance Assessment

Unit theme: Tu día en la escuela

Context for the Integrated Performance Assessment: A group of students from Mexico, including Teresa, is coming to visit your school and attend classes next month. She would like some information about your schedule this year.

Interpretive Task: Watch the *Videohistoria: El primer día de clases* from *Realidades 1, DVD 1, Capítulo 2A.* Write down Teresa's classes by period as she describes her schedule. What time does she have lunch? After the video, write down your classes by period and when you have lunch.

Interpersonal Task: Discuss your schedule with a friend in Spanish class. Ask each other questions to find out what classes you and your friend like and don't like, and explain why.

Presentational Task: Send an e-mail to Teresa. Tell her what class you have each period and when you have lunch. Tell her the classes you like and don't like, and explain why.

Interpersonal Task Rubric

	Score: 1 Does not meet expectations	**Score: 3 Meets expectations**	**Score: 5 Exceeds expectations**
Language Use	Student uses little or no target language and relies heavily on native language word order.	Student uses the target language consistently, but may mix native and target language word order.	Student uses the target language exclusively and integrates target language word order into conversation.
Vocabulary Use	Student uses limited and repetitive language.	Student uses only recently acquired vocabulary.	Student uses both recently and previously acquired vocabulary.

Presentational Task Rubric

	Score: 1 Does not meet expectations	**Score: 3 Meets expectations**	**Score: 5 Exceeds expectations**
Amount of Communication	Student gives limited or no details or examples.	Student gives adequate details or examples.	Student gives consistent details or examples.
Accuracy	Student's accuracy with vocabulary and structures is limited.	Student's accuracy with vocabulary and structures is adequate.	Student's accuracy with vocabulary and structures is exemplary.
Comprehensibility	Student's ideas lack clarity and are difficult to understand.	Student's ideas are adequately clear and fairly well understood.	Student's ideas are precise and easily understood.
Vocabulary Use	Student uses limited and repetitive vocabulary.	Student uses only recently acquired vocabulary.	Student uses both recently and previously acquired vocabulary.

Realidades 

Capítulo 2A **Practice Test**

The High-School Experience in Latin America

1 How does the high-school experience in Latin America compare with that in the United States? There are many similarities, but there are also some noticeable differences.

2 A normal course load for a United States high-school student is usually between five and eight subjects a year, but in Latin America students are more likely to take between ten and twelve. These classes do not, however, meet every day. A class might meet only two or three times a week, which is more similar to schedules in U.S. colleges and universities. As a result, there is more variation in students' day-to-day schedules. In addition, although physical education is taught, team sports are not part of the curriculum. On the other hand, English is mandatory in many schools. Foreign language study is much more common in Latin American schools, and many students speak one or two languages besides Spanish by the time they graduate from high school.

3 Classes in Latin American schools are also structured very differently than those in the United States. Lecturing is the preferred format and there tends to be less student participation. Although extracurricular activities are offered, they are far less common than they are in U.S. schools.

4 It is unusual for Latin American schools to have the amenities, such as lockers, that students in the United States take for granted. As a result, students must carry their backpacks and book bags with them throughout the school day. Latin American students also tend to have much more homework than their U.S. counterparts, so they need these accessories in order to take their books home.

Classes in Latin American schools are also structured very differently than those in the United States. Lecturing is the preferred format and there tends to be less student participation.

5 While letter grades are routinely used in the United States, they are rarely used in Latin America. Although the grading scale varies from country to country, numerical grades, such as 1–10 or 1–20, are the norm.

6 Private schools are common in Latin America and a large number of these are operated by the Roman Catholic Church. Although parochial schools are not usually coeducational, there are many coed private schools that are not affiliated with any church. Because many of these schools are associated with certain ethnic or cultural traditions, students must study the appropriate foreign language, usually American English, German, British English, Italian, or French.

7 One of the most noticeable differences between the U.S. school system and the Latin American one is that students in Latin America are frequently required to wear uniforms. While the uniform is sometimes the same throughout the country, it is more likely identified with a certain school. The girls' uniform is usually a jumper, a blouse, and a tie, or a pleated skirt, a blouse, and a vest or blazer. Boys wear slacks, a shirt and tie, and sometimes a sweater or blazer as well.

Realidades **A**

Capítulo 2A **Practice Test**

Answer questions 1–5. Base your answers on the reading *"The High-School Experience in Latin America."*

1 How does the average number of classes per year compare for U.S. and Latin American students?

- **A** Latin American students take more classes than U.S. students.
- **B** Latin American students take fewer classes than U.S. students.
- **C** Latin American and U.S. students take the same number of classes.
- **D** Latin American and U.S. students take the same number of classes, but in Latin America classes only meet three days a week.

2 Based on the reading, why are backpacks and book bags so important for Latin American students?

- **F** They are expensive and would cost a lot to replace.
- **G** They are a status symbol.
- **H** Latin American students don't have lockers for their books.
- **J** Latin American students don't have shelves for their books.

3 How do church-affiliated schools in Latin America differ from private schools?

- **A** They are usually coeducational.
- **B** They are <u>not</u> usually coeducational.
- **C** They require that students study another language.
- **D** They are not common in Latin America.

4 How does the grading system in Latin America differ from that used in the United States?

- **F** Numerical grades are rarely used.
- **G** Numerical grades are regularly used.
- **H** Letter grades are usually used.
- **J** Letter grades are never used.

5 

Why do you think English is mandatory in Latin American schools? Use details and information from the reading to support your answer.

Realidades A

Nombre ____________________ Fecha ____________

Capítulo 2A

Practice Test Answer Sheet

1 Ⓐ Ⓑ Ⓒ Ⓓ 2 Ⓕ Ⓖ Ⓗ Ⓙ 3 Ⓐ Ⓑ Ⓒ Ⓓ

4 Ⓕ Ⓖ Ⓗ Ⓙ

5

READ THINK EXPLAIN

____

____

____

____

____

____

Realidades A   Nombre ______________________ Fecha ____________

Capítulo 2B   **Reading Skills: Lectura, p. 138**

Locates, Gathers, Analyzes, and Evaluates Written Information

By showing that they can locate, gather, analyze, and evaluate information from one or more reading passages, good readers demonstrate that they know how to conduct research. On a test, readers are often asked to locate, gather, analyze, and evaluate information from a reading passage and then show how to put that information to good use.

Tip

Readers who conduct research often read with a purpose. That means that they are thinking about a research question or problem while they read. If you encounter information in a reading passage that relates to your research question or problem, you should underline or selectively highlight that information. Later, you will come back to the sections that you selectively highlighted to analyze and evaluate the information to determine if it will be useful for your research.

1. On page 138 of your textbook, re-read the **Lectura,** ***El UNICEF y una convención para los niños.*** After you have finished reading, consider the following scenario:

   Imagine that you and some classmates are working on a community service project in which you encourage local students to better appreciate their schools. Now with a pencil, pen, or highlighter, underline the information below from the **Lectura** that might be useful for your project.

   ¿Sabes que es un privilegio estar en una escuela, tener una mochila con libros, unos lápices, una calculadora, unas hojas de papel y un profesor bueno? En ciertas naciones ir a la escuela es difícil o no es possible.

   El UNICEF es la organización internacional de las Naciones Unidas que trabaja para los niños. UNICEF es una sigla inglesa que significa "Fondo Internacional de Emergencia de las Naciones Unidas para los Niños".

   Explain how the information underlined could help you with your community service project.

   ____

   ____

   ____

Sample question:

2. The information in the white sidebar box on page 138 that begins with **"Esta convención dice..."** could best be used
   - **A** to write a report that illustrates the life of underprivileged children.
   - **B** to make a speech demanding that children of any age be given the right to vote.
   - **C** to lead a campaign demanding better treatment for children in a community.
   - **D** to produce a television commercial about the history of UNICEF.

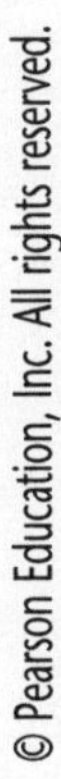

Reading Skills: Perspectivas del mundo hispano, p. 140

Recognizing the Use of Comparison and Contrast

To recognize comparison and contrast in a reading passage, good readers can point out how items or ideas in the reading passage are similar to or different from each other. Sometimes writers will directly state that they are comparing or contrasting items in a reading passage. Other times readers might recognize items in a reading passage that could be compared or contrasted even though the writer might not have presented the information for that purpose.

Tip

With comparison and contrast, one of the biggest challenges for students is to recognize the need to narrow the focus of their comparisons and contrasts. When producing a comparison-contrast chart, you will state things that are obvious. For example, you might choose to compare and contrast apples and oranges and then focus only on the color and shape of the fruits. You then state the obvious: *One is red while the other is orange; both are sort of round in shape*. Professional writers, on the other hand, are less likely to state the obvious. Instead, they aim to teach readers something that readers likely do not already know.

1. On page 140 of your textbook, re-read the **Perspectivas del mundo hispano, *¿Cómo es la escuela?*** After you have finished reading, identify the six features of schools in Spanish-speaking countries that the writer has decided to focus on for comparison and contrast.
   - ways that students ____________ teachers
   - ways that teachers ____________ students
   - ____________
   - use of ____________ time
   - use of ____________
   - number of ____________

Sample question:

2. Based on the information presented in ***¿Cómo es la escuela?***, which statement below is most likely to be true?
   - **A** Students in Spanish-speaking countries are probably more comfortable in class discussions than students in the United States.
   - **B** Students in the United States attend school more days than students in Mexico.
   - **C** Students in the United States and in Spanish-speaking countries are very similar in the ways that they greet and address their teachers.
   - **D** Students in Spanish-speaking countries are accustomed to listening to class lectures.

Realidades **A**

Capítulo 2B

Integrated Performance Assessment

Unit theme: Tu sala de clases

Context for the Integrated Performance Assessment: Your class has decided to assemble packages of school supplies to send to UNICEF so that they can be distributed to a needy school in Latin America. You and your partner have been asked to prepare one package.

Interpretive Task: Read the article on UNICEF on page 138 of *Realidades A* and study the photos. Make a list of 10 items that you think should be included in your package.

Interpersonal Task: Discuss the 10 items that your and your partner listed. From the items that you and your partner listed, select 8 to include in the package.

Presentational Task: Write a note to your teacher telling him/her the 8 supplies you want to include in your package and why.

Interpersonal Task Rubric

	Score: 1 Does not meet expectations	Score: 3 Meets expectations	Score: 5 Exceeds expectations
Language Use	Student uses little or no target language and relies heavily on native language word order.	Student uses the target language consistently, but may mix native and target language word order.	Student uses the target language exclusively and integrates target language word order into conversation.
Vocabulary Use	Student uses limited and repetitive language.	Student uses only recently acquired vocabulary.	Student uses both recently and previously acquired vocabulary.

Presentational Task Rubric

	Score: 1 Does not meet expectations	Score: 3 Meets expectations	Score: 5 Exceeds expectations
Amount of Communication	He/she mentions fewer than 8 items and gives few reasons.	He/she mentions 8 items and gives some reasons.	He/she mentions more than 8 items and gives many reasons.
Accuracy	Student's accuracy with vocabulary and structures is limited.	Student's accuracy with vocabulary and structures is adequate.	Student's accuracy with vocabulary and structures is exemplary.
Comprehensibility	Student's ideas lack clarity and are difficult to understand.	Student's ideas are adequately clear and fairly well understood.	Student's ideas are precise and easily understood.
Vocabulary Use	Student uses limited and repetitive vocabulary.	Student uses only recently acquired vocabulary.	Student uses both recently and previously acquired vocabulary.

Realidades A

Capítulo 2B **Practice Test**

A popular bilingual teen magazine is including a feature in the next issue on what the school day is like for high-school students throughout the United States. Read what this student has to say about a typical day at her school.

Mi día escolar

1 Me llamo Carmen y soy estudiante de la escuela secundaria El Toro en El Toro, California.

2 A las siete y cincuenta de la mañana tengo mi primera clase: español, mi clase favorita. Me gusta hablar español.

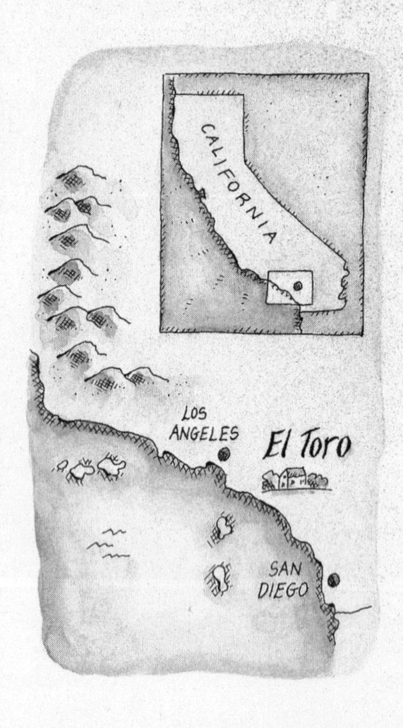

3 En la segunda hora tengo matemáticas. Mi profesora de matemáticas enseña muy bien y me gusta mucho la clase.

4 Mi clase de ciencias es a las nueve y veinte. No tengo mucha tarea en mi clase de ciencias y mi profesor es muy gracioso.

5 En la cuarta hora tengo inglés. Me gusta la clase y mi profesora de inglés es mi profesora favorita.

6 Tengo almuerzo a las diez y cincuenta.

7 En la sexta hora tengo mi clase de literatura. Me gusta mucho leer.

8 Mi clase de educación física es a las doce y veinte. No es mi clase favorita, pero soy deportista y me gusta practicar deportes.

9 En la octava hora tengo historia. A mi profesora de historia le gusta mucho enseñar y es una clase muy interesante.

10 Tengo mi clase de computadoras a la una y cincuenta. No es muy interesante y no me gusta nada.

Realidades A

Capítulo 2B Practice Test

Answer questions 1–5. Base your answers on the reading *"Mi día escolar."*

1 What time does Carmen's first class begin?

- **A** 7:50 A.M.
- **B** 9:20 A.M.
- **C** 10:20 A.M.
- **D** 2:30 P.M.

2 According to the reading, why does Carmen like her math class so much?

- **F** Her teacher doesn't give much homework.
- **G** It's right before lunch.
- **H** She has a very good teacher.
- **J** It isn't difficult for her.

3 Who is Carmen's favorite teacher?

- **A** her Spanish teacher
- **B** her science teacher
- **C** her math teacher
- **D** her English teacher

4 Which class is Carmen's least favorite?

- **F** her computer class
- **G** her science class
- **H** her physical education class
- **J** her history class

5 READ THINK EXPLAIN Based on what you know about Carmen, what kinds of factors influence whether she likes a class or not?

Realidades A | Nombre ______ | Fecha ______

Capítulo 2B

Practice Test Answer Sheet

1 Ⓐ Ⓑ Ⓒ Ⓓ 2 Ⓕ Ⓖ Ⓗ Ⓙ 3 Ⓐ Ⓑ Ⓒ Ⓓ

4 Ⓕ Ⓖ Ⓗ Ⓙ

5

READ
THINK
EXPLAIN

______
______
______
______
______
______

Realidades **A** Nombre ______ Fecha ______

Capítulo 3A **Reading Skills: Actividad 28, p. 167**

Recognizing the Use of Comparison and Contrast

To recognize comparison and contrast in a reading passage, good readers can point out how items or ideas in the reading passage are similar to or different from each other. Sometimes writers will directly state that they are comparing or contrasting items in a reading passage. Other times readers might recognize items in a reading passage that could be compared or contrasted even though the writer might not have presented the information for that purpose.

Tip

The Venn diagram is an excellent visual tool to help you see differences and similarities when comparing and contrasting. The area where two circles overlap is the place to list the similarities between items. In the areas that do not overlap, the differences between items are listed.

1. On page 167 of your textbook, re-read **Actividad 28** *"¿Qué comida hay en el Ciberc@fé @rrob@?"* After you have finished reading, use the Venn diagram below to list the similarities and differences between different menu items.

No. 2 Sincronizadas

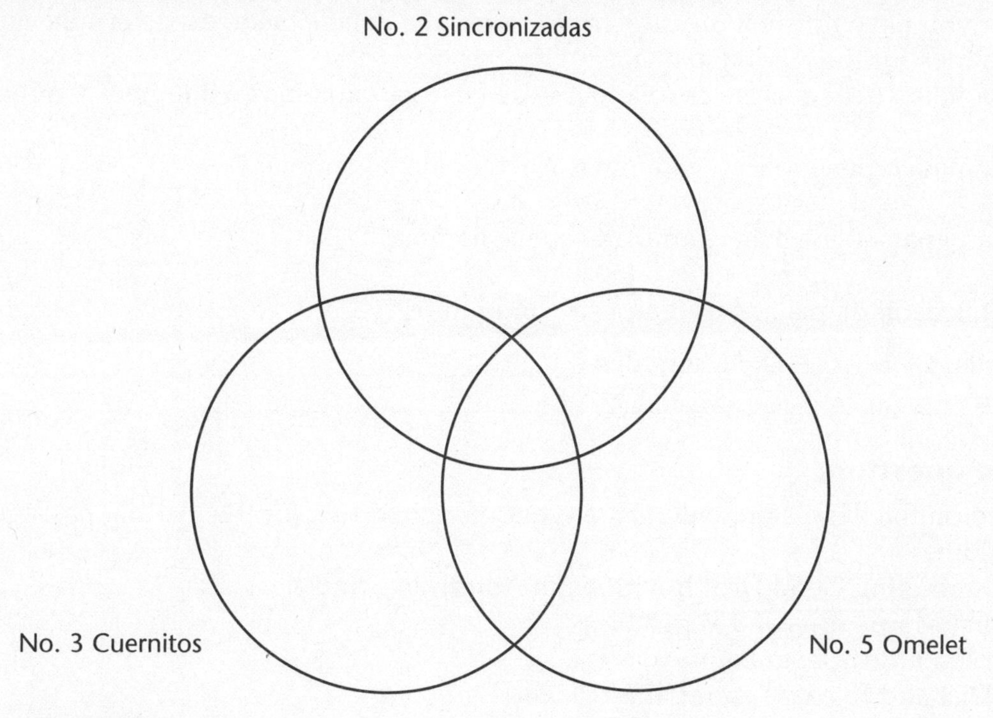

No. 3 Cuernitos

No. 5 Omelet

Sample question:

2. Menu item No. 4, **Chilaquiles,** is different from all the other menu choices because
   A it is the only menu item that costs less than $15.00.
   B it is the only menu item that is offered with *cóctel de fruta.*
   C it is the only menu item that does not contain *jamón.*
   D it is the only menu item that comes with *tortilla de harina.*

Realidades **A** Nombre ____________ Fecha ____________

Capítulo 3A **Reading Skills: Lectura, p. 168**

Determining the Main Idea

To determine the main idea of a reading passage, the reader must be able to describe what a reading passage is about. He or she should be able to summarize the main idea of a reading passage in one sentence. A common problem for students when working with this skill is confusing an important detail in the reading passage with the main idea. Just because something is mentioned in the reading passage does not mean it is the main idea of the passage. Many times the main idea is not even stated in the reading passage. This is often called an implied main idea. No matter if the main idea is stated or implied, the basic question remains the same: "What is this reading passage about?"

One way to determine the main idea of a reading passage is to locate the important details in a passage and then ask yourself, "What do these details have in common?" For some readers, this is like a game of addition: each time a new detail is added, the overall main idea, like the total, must change.

1. On page 168 of your textbook, re-read the **Lectura,** ***Frutas y verduras de las Américas.*** After you have finished reading, try to "add" the details below to determine a possible main idea for the reading passage.

A La pulpa del aguacate es una fuente de energía, proteínas, vitaminas, y minerales.

+

B El mango tiene calcio y vitaminas A y C como la naranja.

+

C La papaya tiene más vitamina C que la naranja.

+

D El licuado de plátano es delicioso y muy nutritivo.

Details A + B + C + D = Main Idea ______________________________

____

Sample question:

2. Based on the details presented above, another good title for the reading passage would be

A "Promoting Good Health with Latin American Fruits."
B "Eat More Fruits and Vegetables."
C "Menu Ideas from Latin America."
D "Diet and Exercise with Latino Flavor."

Integrated Performance Assessment
Unit theme: ¿Desayuno o almuerzo?

Context for the Integrated Performance Assessment: A group of students from San José, Costa Rica is coming to spend two weeks with your Spanish class. You are on the committee that is planning a welcome breakfast for the students.

Interpretive Task: Watch the *Videohistoria: El desayuno from Realidades 1, DVD 2, Capítulo 3A* without the vocabulary words displayed. Decide if the breakfast should be a typical Costa Rican breakfast, an American breakfast, or a combination of both. Make a list of foods that you think the breakfast should include.

Interpersonal Task: Discuss the kind of breakfast and the foods with two or three other members of the breakfast committee. Share your opinion with them and listen to their opinions. Working with the committee, decide on the kind of meal and the food you will have for the welcome breakfast.

Presentational Task: Make an oral presentation to the class explaining the committee's decisions about the welcome breakfast. Include the type of meal and the food you have chosen.

Interpersonal Task Rubric

	Score: 1 Does not meet expectations	**Score: 3 Meets expectations**	**Score: 5 Exceeds expectations**
Language Use	Student uses little or no target language and relies heavily on native language word order.	Student uses the target language consistently, but may mix native and target language word order.	Student uses the target language exclusively and integrates target language word order into conversation.
Vocabulary Use	Student uses limited and repetitive language.	Student uses only recently acquired vocabulary.	Student uses both recently and previously acquired vocabulary.

Presentational Task Rubric

	Score: 1 Does not meet expectations	**Score: 3 Meets expectations**	**Score: 5 Exceeds expectations**
Amount of Communication	Student gives limited or no details about the type of breakfast and the chosen food.	Student gives adequate details about the type of breakfast and the chosen food.	Student gives consistent details about the type of breakfast and the chosen food.
Accuracy	Student's accuracy with vocabulary and structures is limited.	Student's accuracy with vocabulary and structures is adequate.	Student's accuracy with vocabulary and structures is exemplary.
Comprehensibility	Student's ideas lack clarity and are difficult to understand.	Student's ideas are adequately clear and fairly well understood.	Student's ideas are precise and easily understood.
Vocabulary Use	Student uses limited and repetitive vocabulary.	Student uses only recently acquired vocabulary.	Student uses both recently and previously acquired vocabulary.

The Hidden Corn: A Mayan Legend

1 Long ago, corn was hidden inside a large rock and no one knew that it was there. One day, a group of black ants saw a tiny crack in the rock and crawled inside, where they found the corn and tasted it. It was so good that they carried out some kernels to eat later. However, a few of the kernels were too heavy to carry far, so the ants left them behind.

2 Fox came by and found the kernels. He quickly ate them and exclaimed, "How delicious! Now if I could only find some more!" All day long, Fox stayed near the place where he'd found the kernels, looking for more. Finally, when the sun was almost gone and there was just a thin glow of gold left on the horizon, Fox saw the ants making their way to the rock. They entered the tiny crack and later came out loaded down with kernels of corn. After they had left, Fox pried at the crack, but he couldn't get inside the rock. Again he had to be content with eating the kernels the ants could not carry away.

3 When Fox returned home, all the other animals saw how happy and well fed he was. They asked him why, but Fox would not say. So the animals made a plan to find out. That night, they followed Fox to the rock. They saw him eating the corn and they tried it too. "How delicious!" they exclaimed. When they found out that the black ants were bringing the corn out from the rock, they asked them if they would bring out more. The ants agreed but found that they could not bring out nearly enough for all the animals.

4 So the animals asked the red ants and the rat to help, but neither could fit through the crack. Finally, they went to Man and said, "If you will help us, we will give you the secret of this delicious food." Man asked the thunder gods for help, and they sent for Yaluk, the most powerful.

5 Yaluk asked the woodpecker to tap on the thinnest part of the rock and then hide his head. In an instant, Yaluk tossed down a great lightning bolt at the spot where the woodpecker had tapped. The rock burst open, and thousands of golden ears of corn poured out.

6 And so it was that Man and all the animals received the gift of corn. The only unfortunate thing was that when Yaluk threw down his lightning bolt, the woodpecker forgot to hide his head. A piece of rock hit him and his head began to bleed. That is why to this day the woodpecker has a red head.

Capítulo 3A Practice Test

Answer questions 1–5. Base your answers on the reading *"The Hidden Corn: A Mayan Legend."*

1 How did Fox first find the corn?

- A He saw the black ants carrying the kernels.
- B He found some kernels lying on the ground.
- C He saw it through a tiny crack in the rock where it was hidden.
- D He stepped on the rock where it was hidden.

2 At the beginning of the story, Fox and the black ants are the only ones enjoying the gift of corn. Who is enjoying it at the end?

- F the red ants and the rat
- G Yaluk and the other thunder gods
- H Man and all the animals
- J the woodpecker

3 A "just so" story is one in which the events of the story explain a fact of nature, as in "How the Leopard Got His Spots." Which of the following lines from this legend sounds like part of a "just so" story?

- A "Fox pried at the crack, but he couldn't get inside the rock."
- B "Man asked the thunder gods for help."
- C "Yaluk tossed down a great lightning bolt."
- D "The woodpecker has a red head."

4 Why does the writer of this legend call corn a "gift"?

- F Corn was a very important food for the Mayas.
- G Corn is the color of gold.
- H Corn is very rare and needs special conditions to grow.
- J Gift-giving is very important in the Mayan culture.

5 

Choose a passage in this story in which the visual imagery is especially vivid. Explain how the words used in this passage helped to create a clear picture in your mind.

Realidades A

Nombre ____________________ Fecha ____________

Capítulo 3A

Practice Test Answer Sheet

1 Ⓐ Ⓑ Ⓒ Ⓓ 2 Ⓕ Ⓖ Ⓗ Ⓙ 3 Ⓐ Ⓑ Ⓒ Ⓓ

4 Ⓕ Ⓖ Ⓗ Ⓙ

5

READ
THINK
EXPLAIN

Realidades **A** Nombre _______________ Fecha _______________

Capítulo 3B **Reading Skills: Conexiones, p. 197**

Interpreting Diagrams, Graphs, and Statistical Illustrations

When good readers encounter a diagram, graph, or statistical illustration, they are able to make meaning from what they see. In essence, they are able to translate the information that is presented visually or numerically into words. To demonstrate understanding of the information in the diagrams, graphs, or statistical illustrations, readers are often asked to make comparisons involving the information that is presented visually or numerically.

Tip

One strategy that will help you discover the meaning of diagrams or graphs is to practice translating pieces of information from the diagram, graph, or statistics into sentences. In describing what you see, you should become familiar making statements with the following words or expressions:

more than ➔ most ➔ greater than
larger ➔ largest
bigger ➔ biggest
less than ➔ least ➔ fewer than
smaller ➔ smallest
equal ➔ same ➔ different

1. On page 197 in your textbook, review the graph presented in the **Conexiones** section ***"La salud"***. Based on what you see in the graph, complete the sentences below.

The exercise that could possibly burn the most calories for a person between 77 and 82 kilograms would be ___________.

If a person who weighs 55 kilos plays a person that weighs 77 kilos in an hour-long game of tennis, which one will burn more calories? ___________

One hour of ___________ for a person 55–59 kilos could possibly burn the fewest number of calories.

Depending on how hard a person weighing 77–82 kilos plays ___________, the number of calories burned could vary by exactly 100 per cent.

At the lowest level of activity, one hour of ___________ and one hour of ___________ burn the same number of calories for a person weighing 55–59 kilos.

Sample question:

2. If you weighed between 55–59 kilos and wished to burn the largest number of calories in one hour, what would be the best form of exercise for you?

A Dancing at a high level of activity for one hour.
B Playing football or swimming at a high level of activity for one hour.
C Running 10 kilometers in one hour.
D Playing tennis or basketball at a high level of activity for one hour.

Realidades A Nombre ______ Fecha ______

Capítulo 3B **Reading Skills: Lectura, p. 198**

Determining the Main Idea and Identifying Relevant Details

To know the relevant details in a reading passage is to know which ones are most important. The first step in identifying the relevant details is to identify the main idea of the passage. The relevant details are the ones that help support the main idea. After reading a passage, good readers ask themselves, "What is this passage mostly about?" and "Which details in the passage help support, explain, or prove the main idea?"

Tip

Some readers are better able to identify the main idea and the relevant details when they have a graphic organizer. The graphic organizer below presents the main idea as if it were the roof of a house and the relevant details as the columns supporting the roof or main idea.

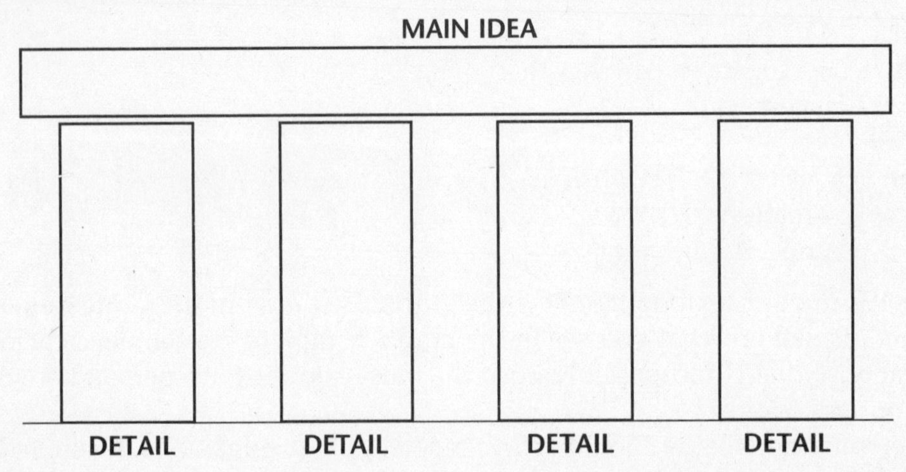

1. On page 198 of your textbook, re-read the **Lectura, *La comida de los atletas.*** After reading, write the statements below in their appropriate place in the above graphic organizer. One statement is irrelevant; it is neither the main idea nor a supporting detail.
   - Para la cena el atleta come papas, carne sin grasa y más verduras y frutas.
   - Los jugadores de fútbol comen comidas equilibradas con muchos carbohidratos, minerales y vitaminas.
   - Carlos Tévez es jugador del equipo Manchester City, un equipo profesional en Inglaterra.
   - La noche antes del partido, el jugador bebe un litro de jugo de naranja.
   - Un jugador típico come mucho pan con mantequilla y jalea, yogur y té.
   - Para el almuerzo antes del partido, come pan, pasta, pollo sin grasa, verduras, frutas y una ensalada.

Sample question:

2. Which statement below does NOT help support the main idea of the **Lectura, *La comida de los atletas*?**
   A Carlos Tévez plays soccer for Manchester City, a professional team in England.
   B The night before a game, a player drinks a liter of orange juice.
   C For dinner, the athlete eats potatoes, lean meat, and more vegetables and fruits.
   D A typical player eats a lot of bread with butter and jelly; yogurt; and tea.

Realidades A

Capítulo 3B

Integrated Performance Assessment

Unit theme: Para mantener la salud

Context for the Integrated Performance Assessment: You are concerned that you are not taking good care of your health. You have decided to make some changes, but you do not know where to start.

Interpretive Task: Listen to a radio announcer as he interviews people about their lifestyles on *Realidades A/B, Audio DVD: Cap. 3B, Track 6.* (Don't worry about the directions given on the DVD itself. Use these directions instead.) As you hear what the people do and eat, decide whether you should or should not do and eat what they do. Make a list of at least 4 ideas you hear under the headings "Debo…" and "No debo…"

Interpersonal Task: You still need some suggestions. Discuss your list of what you should or should not do and eat with your partner. Listen to his/her suggestions. If you hear more good ideas, add them to your list.

Presentational Task: Write a summary of what you should and should not do and eat. There should be at least 5 items in each category.

Interpersonal Task Rubric

	Score: 1 Does not meet expectations	Score: 3 Meets expectations	Score: 5 Exceeds expectations
Language Use	Student uses little or no target language and relies heavily on native language word order.	Student uses the target language consistently, but may mix native and target language word order.	Student uses the target language exclusively and integrates target language word order into conversation.
Vocabulary Use	Student uses limited and repetitive language.	Student uses only recently acquired vocabulary.	Student uses both recently and previously acquired vocabulary.

Presentational Task Rubric

	Score: 1 Does not meet expectations	Score: 3 Meets expectations	Score: 5 Exceeds expectations
Amount of Communication	Student mentions fewer than five things he/she should do and eat and fewer than five things he/she should not do or eat.	Student mentions five things he/she should do and eat and five things he/she should not do or eat.	Student mentions more than five things he/she should do and eat and more than five things he/she should not do or eat.
Accuracy	Student's accuracy with vocabulary and structures is limited.	Student's accuracy with vocabulary and structures is adequate.	Student's accuracy with vocabulary and structures is exemplary.
Comprehensibility	Student's ideas lack clarity and are difficult to understand.	Student's ideas are adequately clear and fairly well understood.	Student's ideas are precise and easily understood.
Vocabulary Use	Student uses limited and repetitive vocabulary.	Student uses only recently acquired vocabulary.	Student uses both recently and previously acquired vocabulary.

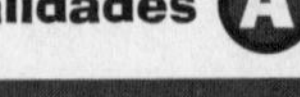

Realidades A

Capítulo 3B **Practice Test**

Pizza, ensaladas y ... helado de fresas

1 Juanito es un chico muy gracioso, inteligente y simpático. Le gusta practicar deportes, jugar videojuegos y montar en bicicleta, pero no le gusta mucho ni ir a la escuela ni estudiar. Y tampoco le gusta comer muchas cosas. Sus comidas favoritas son la pizza, las ensaladas y ... el helado de fresas. Nunca come otras cosas; siempre come pizza, ensaladas y ... helado de fresas. No necesita otras comidas.

2 En el desayuno generalmente come una ensalada de frutas, pero unos días toma una ensalada de papas. En el almuerzo de la escuela come pizza con queso y jamón. Si tiene mucha hambre también toma una ensalada de lechuga y tomates o una ensalada de verduras. Sus amigos quieren compartir sus comidas con él, pero Juanito nunca prueba nuevas comidas. Le encantan las de siempre: la pizza, las ensaladas y ... el helado de fresas.

3 En casa por la noche siempre come lo mismo: pizza (los sábados la come con queso, jamón, judías verdes y cebolla), una ensalada de verduras o frutas y ... un helado de fresas.

4 Todos los días, sin variar: pizza, ensalada y ... helado de fresas. Pero un día ¡no hay ni pizza, ni ensalada ni helado en casa! La mamá de Juanito prepara algo diferente: un sándwich de jamón y queso. Como Juanito tiene MUCHA hambre, prueba un poquito ... ¿Crees que le gusta?

5 Como le gustan las pizzas con jamón y queso ... ¡Le encanta el sándwich de jamón y queso! Ahora Juanito come pizza, ensaladas, helado de fresas y ... sándwiches de jamón y queso.

Practice Test

Answer questions 1–5. Base your answers on the reading *"Pizza, ensaladas y . . . helado de fresas."*

1 How would you describe Juanito?

- **A** He likes to play videogames and study.
- **B** He's a nice kid who likes to read about different foods.
- **C** He's fun to be with, but he spends too much time making pizzas.
- **D** He's a nice kid who doesn't have much variety in his diet.

2 Based on the context, what do you think the word <u>prueba</u> means in paragraph 2?

- **F** shares
- **G** proves
- **H** tries
- **J** prepares

3 Which statement is <u>not</u> true?

- **A** Juanito's friends never want to share their food with him.
- **B** Juanito eats pizza every day.
- **C** Juanito's diet doesn't have much variety.
- **D** Sometimes Juanito has potato salad for breakfast.

4 Juanito never varies the way he has his

- **F** breakfast.
- **G** ice cream.
- **H** pizza.
- **J** salads.

5 READ THINK CREATE Escribe una lista de otros ingredientes para las pizzas de Juanito.

6 

Plan a weekly menu for Juanito—in Spanish—with the foods you think he should be eating. Remember to label the days of the week, the meals of the day, and any snack (*la merienda*) you think Juanito should have.

Realidades A

Nombre ______________________ Fecha ____________

Capítulo 3B

Practice Test Answer Sheet

1 Ⓐ Ⓑ Ⓒ Ⓓ   2 Ⓕ Ⓖ Ⓗ Ⓙ   3 Ⓐ Ⓑ Ⓒ Ⓓ

4 Ⓕ Ⓖ Ⓗ Ⓙ

5

READ THINK EXPLAIN

____
____
____
____
____
____

6

READ THINK EXPLAIN

____
____
____
____
____
____
____
____
____
____

Reading Skills: Conexiones, p. 229

Locates, Gathers, Analyzes, and Evaluates Written Information

By showing that they can locate, gather, analyze, and evaluate information from one or more reading passages, good readers demonstrate that they know how to conduct research. On a test, readers are often asked to locate, gather, analyze, and evaluate information from a reading passage and then show how to put that information to good use.

Tip

Readers who conduct research are skilled at organizing information that they find useful. This means that the readers have a way of putting the information that they find into different categories. Your ability to categorize depends on your ability to see similarities between different pieces of information. Look at these different features of a typical high school below. Which ones would you group together? If you put them into a category, how would you label that category?

A Algebra
B Baseball team
C Community service club
D Debate team
E Earth and space science
F Football team
G Geography
H History

1. On page 229 in your textbook, re-read the **Conexiones,** ***"La historia"*** about Old San Juan. Organize the pieces of information from the reading into two categories. Then, give each category a title.
   A Cristóbal Colón llega a San Juan durante la segunda visita a las Américas en 1493.
   B Los jóvenes pasan el tiempo con sus amigos en los parques, cafés y plazas del Viejo San Juan.
   C En la Catedral de San Juan descansan los restos de Juan Ponce de Léon, famoso explorador de la Florida.
   D El Morro fue construido en el siglo XVI para combatir los ataques de los piratas ingleses y franceses.
   E Mucha gente canta, baila y come en los restaurantes típicos del Viejo San Juan.

   Category 1:
   Title ______________________ includes letters ________
   Category 2:
   Title ______________________ includes letters ________

Sample question:

2. If writing a research paper about the history of San Juan, which information below would NOT be helpful?
   A Cristóbal Colón llega a San Juan durante la segunda visita a las Américas en 1493.
   B Los jóvenes pasan el tiempo con sus amigos en los parques, cafes y plazas del Viejo San Juan.
   C En la Catedral de San Juan descansan los restos de Juan Ponce de Léon, famoso explorador de la Florida.
   D San Juan llega a ser la capital de Puerto Rico en 1521.

Determining the Author's Purpose

To determine the author's purpose for writing a book, a story, an article, or any other text, the reader must figure out why the author wrote that particular book, story, article, or text. Some common purposes for writing are to inform, to entertain, to persuade, or to describe. Readers should also be able to explain why the author uses different techniques or includes different features within a text.

Tip

To figure out the author's purpose, ask yourself these questions:

- Where was this text first published or posted?
- What kinds of people would read this kind of newsletter, advertisement, pamphlet, book, magazine, Web site, text, etc.?
- Why would someone want to read this newsletter, advertisement, pamphlet, book, magazine, Web site, text, etc.?

1. On pages 230–231 in your textbook, re-read the **Lectura,** ***Al centro comercial*** and answer the following questions about the brochure "*¡Vamos a la Plaza del Sol!*"

   Where was this text first published or posted?

   ____

   What kinds of people do you think would read this kind of text?

   ____

   ____

   Why would someone want to read this text?

   ____

   ____

Sample question:

2. What was the author's purpose for publishing the brochure "*¡Vamos a la Plaza del Sol!*"?
   A to inform readers about the different events taking place at the Plaza del Sol shopping center
   B to entertain readers by presenting interesting stories about the Plaza del Sol shopping center
   C to convince readers to buy more products at the Plaza del Sol shopping center
   D to describe how to play Andean music, how to do yoga, how to dance flamenco, and how to make pastries

Realidades A

Capítulo 4A

Integrated Performance Assessment
Unit theme: ¿Adónde vas?

Context for the Integrated Performance Assessment: Your school's Spanish Club is going to Mexico City for a week in January. Among the many activities planned is a visit to the *Plaza del Sol.* In fact, your sponsor has told you that you can all go to the mall on either Saturday or Sunday and on one evening during the week. He/she has formed a committee to select the evening and the weekend day; you are a member of the committee.

Interpretive Task: Read the mall advertisement on pages 230–231 of *Realidades A.* Select the evening and the weekend day you would like to go to the mall. Write your decision on a piece of paper along with why you want to go on those days.

Interpersonal Task: Discuss your opinion and your reasons with the other 2 or 3 members of the committee. Listen to their opinions and reasons. As a group, select the evening and the weekend day for the visits to the mall.

Presentational Task: Make an oral presentation to the members of the Spanish Club announcing when the club will go to the mall and explaining the reasons for the committee's decision.

Interpersonal Task Rubric

	Score: 1 Does not meet expectations	Score: 3 Meets expectations	Score: 5 Exceeds expectations
Language Use	Student uses little or no target language and relies heavily on native language word order.	Student uses the target language consistently, but may mix native and target language word order.	Student uses the target language exclusively and integrates target language word order into conversation.
Vocabulary Use	Student uses limited and repetitive language.	Student uses only recently acquired vocabulary.	Student uses both recently and previously acquired vocabulary.

Presentational Task Rubric

	Score: 1 Does not meet expectations	Score: 3 Meets expectations	Score: 5 Exceeds expectations
Amount of Communication	Student gives limited or no details or reasons.	Student gives adequate details or reasons.	Student gives consistent details or reasons.
Accuracy	Student's accuracy with vocabulary and structures is limited.	Student's accuracy with vocabulary and structures is adequate.	Student's accuracy with vocabulary and structures is exemplary.
Comprehensibility	Student's ideas lack clarity and are difficult to understand.	Student's ideas are adequately clear and fairly well understood.	Student's ideas are precise and easily understood.
Vocabulary Use	Student uses limited and repetitive vocabulary.	Student uses only recently acquired vocabulary.	Student uses both recently and previously acquired vocabulary.

Realidades A

Capítulo 4A **Practice Test**

Aztec Games and Rituals

1 A god of games?! The ancient Aztecs of Mexico had just such a god: Macuilxóchitl (ma-quill-SO-chi-tul), which tells us something about the importance of games in the Aztec culture. And their games were not simply pastimes; they had religious significance as well.

2 *Pelota* was the forerunner of all present-day games that are played with a rubber ball. It was played on a large, H-shaped court. The ball was extremely hard, so hard that the players had to wear padded clothing for protection. They were allowed to hit the ball only with their elbows, hips, and knees. The object of the game was to knock the ball through a stone ring at either end of the court. The team of the first person to succeed in doing this won the game. And it was very important to win, for the team that lost was sacrificed!

3 *Patolli* was a very different type of game, much more enjoyable for all concerned and very popular. It was a board game similar to parcheesi played on a cross-shaped board. Specially marked beans were used as dice. Twelve differently colored counters were divided among the players, who moved them around the board depending upon the throw of the dice.

4 One of the most dramatic of the Aztec rituals was also a ritual for many other indigenous groups. It is still performed by the Totonac of Papantla, a village near Veracruz, Mexico. It is the ancient ritual of the *voladores*, or fliers. It survives to this day because the Spanish missionaries did not forbid it. They did not realize that it was a religious ritual and not just a dangerous sport.

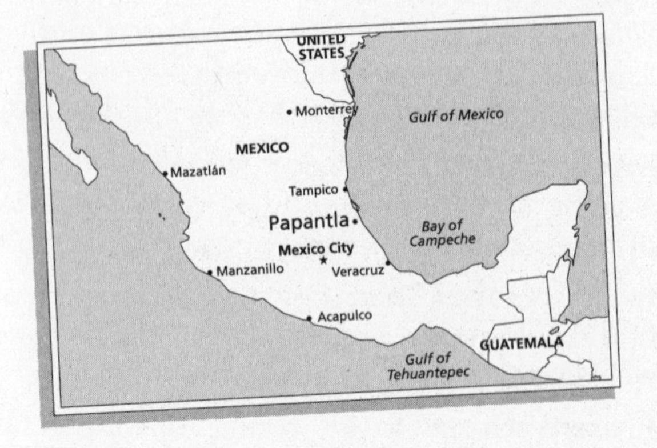

5 Picture a pole a hundred feet high. At its top is a platform on which five men stand in costumes decorated with brightly colored feathers. One man is playing a flute. The other four suddenly leap into the air. You gasp, then realize that each of them is attached to the top of the pole by a rope tied around the ankles. As they fall, the ropes unravel, causing them to circle the pole. The length of the ropes is such that each *volador* flies around the pole thirteen times before landing on the ground.

6 The calendar was at the center of Aztec life. Perhaps the four *voladores* originally represented the four seasons, each with thirteen weeks (the thirteen circuits of the pole). Or the total number of circuits (13) that the *voladores* (4) make may have represented the 52 years that made up a cycle in the ancient sacred calendar. Today, however, it is not the religious aspect of the event, but its spectacular grace and daring that attract spectators.

Practice Test

Answer questions 1–5. Base your answers on the reading *"Aztec Games and Rituals."*

1 The Aztec game of *pelota* has elements of two modern games in it. Which ones?

- **A** soccer and baseball
- **B** basketball and baseball
- **C** volleyball and soccer
- **D** soccer and basketball

2 The Aztec game of *pelota* could still be played today exactly as it was originally, but one element of the game would have to be changed. What is that element?

- **F** The players would have to wear unpadded clothing.
- **G** Both men and women would have to be allowed to play.
- **H** The losing team would have to be allowed to go home after the game.
- **J** The court would have to be shaped like the letter *E*.

3 What present-day sport is most comparable to the ritual of the *voladores?*

- **A** high diving
- **B** bungee jumping
- **C** skateboarding
- **D** rappeling

4 Why can people still see the *voladores* perform today?

- **F** It was not just an Aztec ritual.
- **G** The Spanish missionaries enjoyed the grace and daring of the dangerous sport.
- **H** The missionaries didn't understand what was happening.
- **J** The missionaries encouraged religious rituals.

5 

Imagine that you were alive during the Aztec empire and you observed one of the games or rituals described in this text. Write about your experience attending the event. Include details about the setting, other people who were there, the event itself, and its outcome.

Realidades    Nombre ______________________   Fecha ______________

Capítulo 4A

Practice Test Answer Sheet

1 Ⓐ Ⓑ Ⓒ Ⓓ   2 Ⓕ Ⓖ Ⓗ Ⓙ   3 Ⓐ Ⓑ Ⓒ Ⓓ

4 Ⓕ Ⓖ Ⓗ Ⓙ

5

READ
THINK
EXPLAIN

____
____
____
____
____
____
____
____
____
____

Reading Skills: Actividad 26, p. 258

Identifying Methods of Development and Patterns of Organization

Good readers understand the tools and techniques of authors. To identify the methods of development used by an author in a text, good readers must first determine the author's purpose by asking, "Why was this text written?" After determining the author's purpose, readers next ask, "What techniques did the author use to achieve his or her purpose?" These techniques are known as methods of development and could include, among other things, the organization pattern, the word choice, or the sentence structure used in the text.

Tip

To understand the methods of development used by authors, it helps to start thinking like a writer. Imagine how your writing would change depending on the different purposes you had as a writer. For example, think about cars and all the reasons you might have to write about them. How would you write an advertisement to sell a used car? Would your writing techniques change or stay the same if you were helping complete a police report about a car accident that you witnessed? What would happen to those writing techniques if your purpose for writing was to request information from a manufacturer about electric cars? Would those same techniques work in a speech to convince your parents to lend you their car for the entire weekend?

1. On page 258 in your textbook, re-read **Actividad 26 *"La ciudad deportiva"*** and answer the following questions about the advertisement, *"Mi sueño."*

What do you think was the author's purpose for writing this text?

____

____

What techniques does the author use to achieve his purpose? Think about the way that the text is organized, the types of sentences used, and the words chosen.

____

____

____

____

Sample question:

2. Which technique below is NOT used by the author in composing *"Mi sueño"*?

A He lists all his accomplishments as a professional athlete to impress his customers.
B He portrays himself as someone willing to share his good fortune with others.
C He describes his facilities and staff as being of the highest quality.
D He shows himself to be dedicated to his primary customers: families and children.

Realidades **A** Nombre ______________________ Fecha ______________

Capítulo 4B **Reading Skills: Lectura, pp. 260–261**

Recognizing the Use of Comparison and Contrast

To recognize comparison and contrast in a reading passage, good readers can point out how items or ideas in the reading passage are similar to or different from each other. Sometimes writers will directly state that they are comparing or contrasting items in a reading passage. Other times readers might recognize items in a reading passage that could be compared or contrasted even though the writer might not have presented the information for that purpose.

Tip

After reading a text in which the author uses comparison and contrast, it is helpful for the reader to restate what he or she read using some of these common expressions:

______________________, but ______________________.
______________________; however, ______________________.
______________________. On the other hand, ______________________.
Although ______________________, ______________________.
While ______________________, ______________________.
Both ______________________ and ______________________.
______________________. Similarly, ______________________.
______________________. Likewise, ______________________.

1. On pages 260–261 in your textbook, re-read the **Lectura, *Sergio y Paola: Dos deportistas dotados.*** Then, fill in the blanks of the sentences below with information that shows how Sergio and Paola are both similar and different.

   With regard to interests, both Sergio and Paola ______________________
   ______________________.

   Sergio won his first professional tournament when he was 17 years old. Similarly, Paola ______________________.
   Regarding their goals, ______________________.
   Paola ranks among the best platform divers in the world. Likewise, Sergio ________
   ______________________.

Sample question:

2. Which statement below is true about Sergio and Paola?
   A Both of them won their first professional competitions before they were eighteen years old.
   B Both of them have been competing since they were three years old.
   C While Paola enjoys spending time with her family, Sergio enjoys camping.
   D Paola wants to win a gold medal in the Olympics, while Sergio wants to be the #1 golfer in the world.

Realidades A

Capítulo 4B

Integrated Performance Assessment
Unit theme: ¿Qué te gusta hacer?

Context for the Integrated Performance Assessment: A group of students from Madrid is coming to spend two weeks in your school. They would like to know if American students do the same activities on Saturdays that Spanish students do.

Interpretive Task: Watch the *Videohistoria: ¡A jugar!* from *Realidades 1, DVD 2, Capítulo 4B* (without the vocabulary words displayed) in which several students from Madrid talk about their Saturday activities. Make a list of these activities.

Interpersonal Task: Compare your list with your partner's list to make sure that you both know what the Spanish students do on Saturdays. Work with your partner to add a list of activities that American students often do on Saturdays.

Presentational Task: Write an e-mail to one of the students from Madrid comparing the activities students in Spain and the U.S. do on Saturdays. Be sure to include similarities and differences.

Interpersonal Task Rubric

	Score: 1 Does not meet expectations	**Score: 3 Meets expectations**	**Score: 5 Exceeds expectations**
Language Use	Student uses little or no target language and relies heavily on native language word order.	Student uses the target language consistently, but may mix native and target language word order.	Student uses the target language exclusively and integrates target language word order into conversation.
Vocabulary Use	Student uses limited and repetitive language.	Student uses only recently acquired vocabulary.	Student uses both recently and previously acquired vocabulary.

Presentational Task Rubric

	Score: 1 Does not meet expectations	**Score: 3 Meets expectations**	**Score: 5 Exceeds expectations**
Amount of Communication	Student gives little information about the similarities and differences between the activities of students in Spain and the U.S.	Student gives some information about the similarities and differences between the activities of students in Spain and the U.S.	Student gives much information about the similarities and differences between the activities of students in Spain and the U.S.
Accuracy	Student's accuracy with vocabulary and structures is limited.	Student's accuracy with vocabulary and structures is adequate.	Student's accuracy with vocabulary and structures is exemplary.
Comprehensibility	Student's ideas lack clarity and are difficult to understand.	Student's ideas are adequately clear and fairly well understood.	Student's ideas are precise and easily understood.
Vocabulary Use	Student uses limited and repetitive vocabulary.	Student uses only recently acquired vocabulary.	Student uses both recently and previously acquired vocabulary.

Una conversación difícil

1 Es viernes y son las siete de la noche. Generalmente me gusta estar con mis amigos los fines de semana. ¿Adónde vamos mis amigos y yo? Al centro comercial. Al cine. Al parque, donde jugamos al fútbol americano o, en el invierno, al gimnasio, donde jugamos al básquetbol o al vóleibol.

2 Pero mañana, no. Mañana me gustaría ir de pesca con papá. Es un día muy especial: es su cumpleaños.

—¿Papá?

—¿Sí, Roberto?

—Papá, me gustaría...

—Sí, Roberto. Te gustaría ir al parque. Lo siento, pero estoy cansado.

—No, papá. Quiero ir al campo con...

—A ver... Quieres ir al campo con Ramón y su familia mañana. Estoy ocupado, Roberto. Puedes hablar con tu mamá...

—¡No, no, papá! Quiero ir de pesca...

—¿De pesca? ¿Cómo vas a ir de pesca? No puedes ir solo. ¿Con quién vas a ir de pesca?

—Contigo, papá. Quiero pasar el día de tu cumpleaños contigo.

—¿Conmigo? ¿Mi cumpleaños? ¡No me digas!

—¿No vas a estar ni cansado ni ocupado, papá?

—No, no, Roberto. ¿Quién puede estar cansado en su cumpleaños? Pero sí voy a estar ocupado. Voy a ir de pesca contigo.

Practice Test

Answer questions 1–6. Base your answers on the reading *"Una conversación difícil."*

1 What does <u>*cumpleaños*</u> mean in paragraph 2?

- **A** vacation
- **B** birthday
- **C** free time
- **D** a kind of park

2 What is different about this weekend?

- **F** Roberto is going to the mall with his friends.
- **G** Roberto is going either to the park or to the gym with his friends.
- **H** It is Roberto's birthday.
- **J** It is Roberto's father's birthday.

3 Why doesn't Roberto's father want to go to the park?

- **A** He's tired.
- **B** He's sick.
- **C** He's busy.
- **D** It's Friday evening.

4 Why does Roberto want to go to the country?

- **F** He wants to be with Ramón and his family.
- **G** He wants to go fishing with his father.
- **H** He can talk to his mother there.
- **J** It's his birthday.

5 Which of the following is the best reason why Roberto's father is so happy at the end of the story?

- **A** He loves to go fishing.
- **B** He isn't tired or busy anymore.
- **C** Roberto wants to spend the day with him.
- **D** Tomorrow is his birthday.

6 

This year Roberto may not have bought his father a birthday present. As far as his father is concerned, however, Roberto is giving him the best gift possible. There is a common English expression that says, "It's the thought that counts." Briefly explain this expression in relation to the story and give an example from your own experience.

Realidades A

Nombre ____________________ Fecha ____________

Capítulo 4B

Practice Test Answer Sheet

1 Ⓐ Ⓑ Ⓒ Ⓓ 2 Ⓕ Ⓖ Ⓗ Ⓙ 3 Ⓐ Ⓑ Ⓒ Ⓓ

4 Ⓕ Ⓖ Ⓗ Ⓙ 5 Ⓐ Ⓑ Ⓒ Ⓓ

6

READ
THINK
EXPLAIN

Notes

Notes

Notes

Notes